What You See Is What You Get

What You See Is What You Get

Desktop publishing and the production revolution at Cambridge University Press 1980 – 1996

Tom O'Reilly

PAGE D'OR
MMXX

Page d'Or is an imprint of Prosperity Education Limited
Registered offices: 58 Sherlock Close, Cambridge CB3 0HP,
United Kingdom

A catalogue record for this book is available from the British Library

ISBN: 978-1-9161297-9-5

Typeset in Times New Roman 10pt by ORP Cambridge

For further information visit: www.pagedor.co.uk

Ad infinitum et ultra.

For Liam and Elise

Contents

CBML code set in letterpress by Elizabeth Fraser. Photo © Damian Penfold.

Preface

The research for this book was conducted in 2012 and the findings submitted as a dissertation essay for an MA in Publishing Studies at Anglia Ruskin University, Cambridge.

On re-reading, eight years later, the transcripts of the oral histories that formed part of the study, I was struck again by the detailed, first-person accounts of the great changes made to the processes and technologies of Cambridge University Press between the years 1980 and 1996. This was the time when the mechanics of content production became fully digitised and its workflows were revolutionised, and when the leaders of the Press sought to innovate in preparation for an unknown future in academic publishing.

In order to gain a comprehensive understanding of this aspect of Press history, six key members of staff, past and present, were interviewed, gathering perspectives from: the period's Publishing Operations Director; the Academic & Professional (AcPro) Books Production Manager; an AcPro text designer; the Managing Director of the Technical Applications Group (TAG) and mainstream Composition; a prepress technician; and the first desktop-publishing typesetter to be employed by the Press.

By using Cambridge University Press as a case study, the book reflects on the content-production efforts of the academic publishing industry, in which the Press remains a leading player. The hypothesis is that the introduction of desktop publishing and, later, the standardised pdf printing medium, provided an economic distraction to the Press' existing, in-house realisation of the future importance of generically encoded Academic Book content.

From the outset, the work had two objectives:

1. To chart the origins and subsequent evolution of the technologies and innovations behind contemporary content production in academic publishing.
2. To understand how these technologies were adopted by the Printing and Publishing divisions of Cambridge University Press.

Two of the five internal chapters concern the development and convergence of multiple technologies, detailing the chronological and functional aspects of each innovation to chart their integration in to the Press' operational processes. There follows a reflective description of the Academic Book Divisions' design, typesetting and prepress production processes in place prior to 1996, and a comparative review of the production workflows in place in 1996, by when desktop publishing, digital page-layout technologies, and on-screen WYSIWYG editing applications had entered the design, typesetting and prepress processes.

While there is additional scope for research into the cultural and Press-political aspects of the subject, as well as the direct relationship between technological change and the organisation's financial revenue, the parameters of this book are confined to detailing the chronological series of events that have led to present-day Academic Book production processes, and to reflecting on how and why and to what effect these changes were implemented at Cambridge University Press during the period 1980–1996.

The basis of this endeavour is represented in the following questions:

When did raster imaging and laser printing enter the production workflow, and how did these technologies effect the existing processes of design, typesetting and prepress production?

What benefits and disadvantages did desktop publishing bring to the Press, and how did it impact upon external suppliers and internal composition processes?

How did the Press go about encoding its content, enabling future multi-format publishing, and when was this need for capturing reusable data first realised?

Privileged access to as-yet uncatalogued content of the Press archive resulted in the discovery of original sources from which descriptions of early Printing House procedures and acquisitions were obtained. In Chapter Three, for instance, the 1980 Computer Aided Composition workflow is detailed by reference to archived flow charts and summaries thereof using the following system, which was devised in collaboration with the Press archivist, Dr Rosalind Grooms:

In-text citation: (Archive A)
Full reference: Simplified CAC Operation Process Chart. ULC UA Accn: 2009/47/21, Cambridge University Press papers.

In-text citation: (Archive B)
Full reference: Revised Cost Rate: CAC. ULC UA Accn: 2009/47/21, Cambridge University Press papers.

In-text citation: (Archive C)
Full reference: CAC Procedure. ULC UA Accn: 2009/47/21, Cambridge University Press papers.

By the disclosure in an indexed appendix of complete transcripts of the interviews conducted, the reader is provided with the original source of referential material cited and representative, first-hand accounts of the period in question. When citing these

3

sources the book employs, by way of example, the following system of reference:

In-text citation: (App. A, p.52)
Full reference: Appendix A: Transcript of interview with Michael Holdsworth, p.52).

A concise biographical description of each interviewee precedes the interview transcripts on Page 50.

Introduction

Book production at Cambridge University Press, the world's oldest publisher and longest continual printer, has evolved with the industry, adapting at its forefront to successive technological shifts throughout a four-hundred-year manufacturing legacy[1]. Perhaps surprisingly, given such a vast period of time, there have been just two major changes to the process by which text is prepared prior to being mechanically printed on paper.

Johannes Gutenburg's publishing innovation of 1450, by which the setting of individual characters of metal type in braces or matrices enabled for the first time the mass-production of printed sheets of text, remained until the second half of the nineteenth century the fundamental production standard.

The introduction of phototypesetting in the 1950s[2] and the increasing popularity across the industry in printing by offset lithography saw an end to almost half a millennium of letterpress typesetting as the primary service offered by Cambridge Printing[3]. By the time laser-printing technology was adopted in the late-1970s[4], phototypesetting machines utilised pre-digitised fonts that were stored either in computer memory or on magnetic disk[5]. By the end of the decade, they had become fully electronic 'imagesetters': devices controlled by Graphical User Interfaces and capable of outputting text and graphics together by employing a raster-image processor to control the etching of pixels by laser beam on to a photoreceptive print carrier.

By the end of the 1980s, PostScript-fed, raster-image processing had rendered the purely photomechanical process near obsolete. Within five years the industry had irreversibly changed, and with it the way books were produced by Cambridge University Press.

With inflation peaking at twenty-two per cent in 1980, and UK unemployment reaching an unprecedented three million by January 1982 (12.1 per cent of the working population), this period of dramatic technological change saw the entire British manufacturing industry effectively disintegrate (Bain and Gennard, 1995, p.160): economic recession on a global scale, cuts in educational funding, restrictions in library budgets, and overcapacity in the UK printing industry saw the demise of many UK prepress and printing firms (Black, 1992, p.55). In 1982 British printers were competing against prices quoted by overseas printers that were as much as 45 per cent below the existing British 'costs only' prices. Already, it had become possible for a book to be typeset in one country and printed and bound in another (Bain and Gennard, 1995, p.161). The introduction by the Conservative Party of the Employment Acts of 1980 and 1982, which narrowed the definition of a lawful trade dispute between workers and employers to matters wholly or mainly employment-related, gave rise to vigilant yet ultimately futile union efforts (in the form of the National Graphical Association (NGA), covering the printers, and the Society of Graphical and Allied Trades (SOGAT), covering dispatch, distribution, and clerical workers) to fortify the industry's domestic employment situation (Needle, 2004, p.115). The British newspaper industry provides a stark instance of how desperate a time this was when, in 1986, the transition of production methods from hot metal to Computer Aided Composition (CAC), despite fierce union resistance, literally occurred overnight[6].

In contrast, during this time, Cambridge University Press, under the leadership of Sir Geoffrey Cass, (Chief Executive Officer, 1972–1992, and University Printer, 1982–83 and 1991–92), enjoyed a virtually unbroken record of success in terms of consolidation and expansion (Black, 1992, p.55). With its maintenance of 'a strong financial reserve, continuous investment in high-quality publishing projects, and progressive development of a global marketing strategy', the Press was, in Cass' words, 'a rock around which swirl the currents of mergers, takeovers and failures in the printing and publishing industry' (Black, 1992, p.57)[7]. By 1984, having produced approximately eight-million units of book, the Press was the largest, purely academic publisher in the United Kingdom (Black, 1984, p.305)[8]. By 1987, two years before the closure of the printing operation of Oxford University Press, Cambridge was outputting 1,000 new academic and educational titles a year, two thirds of which were being exported to more than 150 countries worldwide, an accomplishment for which it received The Queen's Award for Export Achievement (Black, 1984, p.58).

The success of the Press during a time when its competitors largely floundered may be attributed to a foresight with regard to the era's technological developments, and to a decision to economise its printing operations accordingly. With print runs severely reduced, the Printing Division focused on investing in efficient new technologies in order to reduce machine setting-up times in comparison to their running times. At the end of the 1970s, and understanding the principles and potential of rasterised laser imaging, Cambridge Printing was one of the first printers to incorporate the Monotype Lasercomp imagesetter into its composition workflow[9]. Considered to be the first commercial raster-imaging typesetting machine, the Lasercomp was itself a technological revolution and is arguably responsible, at least in part, for the seismic transition that was to follow.

The introduction of computerised word processing, the Graphical User Interface, and the convergence of this technology with that of photocomposition, imagesetting and, later, platesetting technologies meant that authorial text could be created and stored digitally, revised easily, and coded generically to be reconstituted in multiple typefaces and fonts prior to publication. The way in which manuscripts were produced and submitted had changed: from its inception through to its manufacture, the book had become a fully digitised product. The concept of 'create once/ publish many' has led to print being just one format of the contemporary production process (Phillips, 2007, p.548).

In order to understand how these recent advancements were achieved, and how they contributed to the present-day methods of book production, we should first look at how content has been processed since the days of letterpress composition.

1

Electronic markup:
control codes for defining text

All forms of writing require 'markup', or data to be added to the text of a document that convey instruction regarding its structure and appearance when output: it separates the logical elements of the text and specifies the processing functions to be performed on those elements (Goldfarb, 1981, p.1).

At a very basic level, 'punctuational' markup exists in the spaces between words, indicating word boundaries, in commas indicating phrasal boundaries, and in full stops to indicate sentence boundaries (Coombs, Renear and DeRose, 1987, p.935). At the basic 'presentational' level, by way of example, an author may indicate the start of a new paragraph by inserting a full line space followed by a certain amount of horizontal space, or use full caps to denote an internal heading. 'Markup is not part of the text or content of the expression, but tells us something about it' (Coombs, Renear and DeRose, 1987, p.934). Prior to the computerisation of the printing industry in the 1960s, markup instruction for the typesetter was administered, by hand, by text designers and copy-editors working on an author's manuscript. By using a standardised set of codes and language, text could be accurately prepared for typesetting as long as the typesetting system to be used – and therefore its typefaces – was known in advance. With the convergence of computing, typesetting, and word processing in the 1980s, authors began to produce electronic text instead of mechanically typed manuscripts, and as a result many text-formatting languages were created with the intention of simplifying this specific task. These varying approaches to typesetting markup may be generally classified as 'procedural' and 'descriptive'.

Procedural markup

Procedural or 'specific' markup is a device-dependent coding structure that consists of commands indicating how text should be output, and it is generally associated solely with formatting and presentation when printed.

Most word-processing, procedural markup languages are proprietary, print-focused packages that are typically incompatible between programmes. Once a document's text has been encoded, it is confined to being processed by the software with which it was created. The obvious limitations of this language resulted in publishers devising ingenious ways of bringing conformity to the authorial content being submitted.

Two such alternative approaches to inserting specific, typographical markup into a text document are:

Off-line typesetting or disk-conversion

Due to the high prices demanded by typesetting vendors for proprietary compositors' workstations, and in a popular attempt to process the many different versions of formatted text being supplied, typesetters used software programmes to prepare files for conversion to their own typesetting systems. Due to the variance in text-formatting languages in circulation, this process required considerable intervention post-conversion in order to attain accuracy.

Vendor-independent typesetting codes

In a variation of the off-line method, sets of intermediate, industry-standard coding were devised to circumvent the costly problem of typesetter dependence. Such common typographical markup, embedded by the author within the text of a document, can be converted to vendor-specific codes at a later stage in the book-production process, thus freeing the publisher from having to commit to a specific typesetting system. Adobe's PostScript and

TeX[10] are just two notable examples of such procedural printer-control markup[11].

Descriptive markup

In contrast to procedural markup, which focuses on how a document should appear when output, descriptive, or 'generic' markup is concerned with content: describing or 'tagging' the individual editorial components, or elements, of a document's structure, 'identifying a textual feature of some kind' (Renear, 2003).

While procedural markup specifies a particular process to be applied to a document component, descriptive markup indicates what that component is (Pitti, 2002). If the individual components of a document are known (e.g. Chapter number, chapter title, paragraph, quotation, reference, footnote, etc.) the desired typographic and formatting styles – i.e. the procedural coding – can be applied and, importantly, reconfigured later by any number of processors.

Generic markup evolved from the macro principal of procedural 'printer control' coding, and it is credited to a 1967 presentation by William W. Tunnicliffe entitled 'The separation of information content of documents from their format', which led to his 1970s development of GenCode, a standard aimed specifically at the publishing industry[12]. A simultaneous, speculative paper by Stanley Rice, a New York book designer, entitled 'Standardising editorial structures', added appeal to the theory, and led to a movement focused on separating a document's formatting from its content in order to maximise its publishing potential.

From its GenCode origins, generic coding has undergone several transformations throughout its history; from GML, to SGML, and from HTML to XML, each new language a derivative of the last, adapting to developments made in the 'information age' that have enabled modern, cross-platform content distribution as we know it today.

11

GML and SGML

Based on the ideas of Tunnicliffe and Rice, GML, or 'generalised markup language', was devised by Charles F. Goldfarb in 1969 and published by IBM[13], which at the time was conducting research into integrated law-office information systems, and sought to employ GML as an efficient document-processing tool: specifically, as a coding structure that could be read by both machines and humans. In addition to tagging a document's individual components, GML introduced the concept of 'a formally defined document type with an explicit nested structure' (Goldfarb, 1990, p.2).

A Document Type Definition, or DTD, accompanies each GML-encoded document, defining for the benefit of the output platform the validity of its elements. In validating the coded elements, a DTD states the hierarchy in which each tag is to be presented, according to the GML, and provides nomenclature for naming those elements so that they can be accurately processed by the typesetter or output device. To ensure that a document encoded in GML matches the corresponding DTD, a parsing programme is run to assess the quality and conformity of the markup. An allowance for 'nested' elements in the GML code means that an already tagged element can be processed differently, depending on its position within a document[14]. However, DTD notation does not define procedural markup, such as styling or formatting: instead, it is parsed, according to the owner's rules, in order to validate the structure of an encoded document. Importantly, one DTD can be used to validate the content of multiple documents being published by an organisation.

In 1978, the American National Standards Institute (ANSI) enlisted Goldfarb to work with the GenCode Committee in creating a text-description language standard based on GML (Goldfarb, 1990, p.2). Standardised General Markup Language, or SGML, was designed as an 'unambiguous format for text interchange and an ASCII[15] markup language rich enough to permit future processing' (Watson, 2005, p.5), the aim being to publish an open-standard process that would accurately and quickly convert electronic documents between computers and output devices. The first draft of the Standardised General Markup Language was published in 1980 and was adopted by several major organisations, such as the US Department of Defense and Internal Revenue Service, thus popularising the format with immediate effect. However, it took some years and much review of the code before it was granted its International Standard approval in 1986, and several further transmutations before it became a true application standard in publishing.

HTML and XML

A derivative of SGML, HTML, or Hypertext Markup Language[16], brought the coding of content to the internet by 'defining the information structure of web pages' (Taylor, 1996, p.11), ultimately creating the World Wide Web. Yet, unlike SGML, it is in fact concerned more with formatting than structure. While SGML-encoded text is accompanied by a detailed DTD, authored by the publisher depending on the desired output, HTML is just one application of SGML containing comparatively fewer tags, and as such it does not require a bespoke DTD because web browsers can by definition recognise them (Taylor, 1996, p.11). Technically, it is itself an SGML DTD, limited to 'simple procedural coding dedicated to online display and hypermedia linking' (Pitti, 2002). By embedding within its structure 'hypertext' links, HTML includes a referential feature, enabling the reader to move between HTML files, images, and other multimedia programmes across the internet (Burrows, 1999, p.9).

A reason why generic markup such as HTML is necessary for presenting content in web pages is that the content must be device-independent. Variables such as line breaks and font size are ultimately determined by the width of a browser's window or the viewing device's screen. However, HTML's ability to display generically marked-up content on-screen is undermined by its inability to organise the content online so that it can be structurally accessed and electronically exchanged, or *repurposed*, elsewhere. In response to this limited application of HTML, Extensible Markup Language, or XML, was introduced by the World Wide Web Consortium (W3C) in 1998 as a 'meta language', a language to generate languages. As with GML, SGML and HTML, tagged information in an XML-encoded document accompanied by a DTD can be parsed to produce multiple outputs. However, being extensible, and in contrast to HTML's fixed tagging, a new data-exchange language can be created by defining the XML structure and tags. By using different stylesheets denoting format and typographic style, a single XML source code can produce multiple outputs, or languages, including those used to generate print pdfs. Regardless of the textual content of an XML-encoded document, every occurrence of output, when processed, will be rendered identically, due to its implementation of Unicode, the universal character-set standard maintained by the Unicode Consortium. This failsafe approach to character encoding and strict rule sets defining specific markup-language DTDs, are just two attributes of XML that have helped to make it today the generic coding structure employed by virtually every large-scale publisher of academic content in the world. However, its long journey has encountered competition along the way, most notably in the combination of binary word processing and graphical computer-display technologies.

Presentational 'WYSIWYG' markup

Despite its acceptance by the industry as a progressive advance in electronic-text handling, SGML – the complex coding and exhaustive markup rules of which demanded considerable effort and set-up cost prior to any authorial text being written – did not become the standard it had promised. It was in fact best suited to organisations, such as the military and certain governmental departments, for whom management of vast and complex amounts of content was important, and who could include the format as an obligatory part of their operational procedures. It was not until XML, the evolution of HTML, was published as an open standard in 1998 that publishers realised the full importance of generic markup as a sensible means of preparing content for dissemination across multiple platforms, including those that had yet to be invented. However, by then an alternative method of procedural markup, which did not require the expertise and up-front financial commitment inherent to SGML, had already established itself as the new typesetting system of choice.

By the time SGML was awarded its International Standard approval in 1986, the emergence had occurred of WYSIWYG (What You See Is What You Get) word-processing technology, in which the procedural coding of a document's content became hidden to the user beneath the Graphical User Interface of a personal computer. This development had resurrected procedural markup to be, for many, the only coding standard necessary to produce content for the publishing process. Software applications such as WordStar, WordPerfect, XyWrite, Microsoft Word, and, later, MacWrite, brought the text-processing functionality of stand-alone word processors to within the hardware of a personal computer and its accompanying desktop printing device. Each of the rival processes at the time utilised 'batch processing', a method by which markup is processed for output all in one go (Taylor, 1996, p.8) – decisions effecting line and page breaks, for instance, were made at this point – meaning the user could only view the formatted content when it was output to paper. By having immediate, visual feedback of the markup being applied to a document *as it was created*, the user gained a hitherto inexperienced level of typographic control. More importantly, extensive page-description languages and the development of 'non-impact' laser-printing technology in the early 1980s allowed, for the first time, a complex mixture of text and graphics to be assembled on-screen and printed at near-camera-ready quality

(Oakley and Norris, 1988, p.1). The savings in production overheads to publishers, and the technical enlightenment afforded to authors and designers alike, put a temporary end to efforts in the generic coding of multi-purposed content and, at a time of global depression, focused the industry instead on producing quicker, cheaper, and simpler output to paper.

'Desktop Publishing' had arrived.

2

Desktop publishing:
the revolution comes

Desktop publishing is the result of a timely convergence of four symbiotic technologies: page-description programming, raster-image processing, laser printing, and the Graphical User Interface; and its success in revolutionising not only the publishing prepress process but also electronic office communications can be credited to the belief and encouragement of an individual.

Jonathan W. Seybold, the revered 'father of computer type-setting', was a pioneer in developing computer applications and typesetting systems for the printing and publishing industries. His company, Rocappi, was founded in 1963 and, from the outset, its vision was one of technological advancement of the way in which computers could aid the mechanical printing process[17]. In 1971 Seybold launched *The Seybold Report*, a newsletter published amongst the publishing and design communities that documented in real time the industry's move towards digital revolution. It was this authoritative and influential reputation that placed him at the centre of the era's innovative core, providing a neutral observation point from which the concurrent development of many new technologies could be witnessed.

Beginning in 1981, and ending shortly after his death in 2004, the Seybold Seminars were biannual conferences and trade shows held for the electronic publishing, printing, and graphics in-dustries, and, for almost a quarter of a century, they charted the progress, present and future, of digital technologies. By the inau-gural conference in 1981, Seybold had become synonymous with computer typesetting and closely acquainted with the industry's key players and emerging innovations. Fascinated by advances being made in the newspaper industry (whereby for some time computer programmes had performed automatic, albeit relatively crude, hyphenation of text in prepress composition), he realised that computer coding could in theory drive the wider process of 'preparation, correction, manipulation and formatting of written text' for the entire publishing gamut[18].

In 1984, having surmised that the difficulties lay in producing aesthetically pleasing font output to rival and commercially succeed that of conventional phototypesetters, Seybold observed that (1984, p.373):

The more closely a system tries to approximate the true output type fonts on a display screen, and the more manipulation of line art and pictures which it permits, the more difficult it will be to support a variety of output image processors.

At the time, every typesetting manufacturer's output devices worked differently to one another: each phototypesetting machine contained different fonts, their unique selections making ownership of such equipment a limiting experience in terms of potential output, and the binary coding by which these fonts were incorporated into text would differ, greatly, between devices.

Investing in any one system was not only an expensive process but also a bind – a reliance on the manufacturer should anything go wrong – and a confinement to whatever proprietary fonts came with the machine.

By standardising a resolution-independent way of processing on-screen data to a universal output device, the limitations, costs, and efficiencies of printing would be reduced, and the opportunity for creating just one set of code for use in multiple typesetting machines would simplify the entire print, production, and pre-press processes immeasurably.

Adobe PostScript

PostScript is a page-descriptive programming language, or PDL, able to describe text as well as graphics on one page and precisely communicate this information between computer and an output device, regardless of its resolution capability. A PostScript-empowered document containing text and images is specified by vector graphics: mathematic algorithms consisting of straight lines and Bézier curves that are digitally converted, or rasterised, into dots ready for printing. Its origins, like so many computer-led technological advancements of the 1970s and 1980s, can be sourced to the Xerox PARC research and development company in Palo Alto, California. It was there that John Warnock and Charles Geschke began their work on standardising page-description code, a pursuit they considered essential for the future of office communications, the market in which Xerox, having developed the first laser printer in 1981, was a chief player. Originating in the 1970s, the first PARC page-description language was named 'Press', which, by the end of the decade, under the development of Warnock and Geschke, had evolved into the more sophisticated 'Interpress'. Though this language was considered at the time by the Silicon Valley research community as a communications breakthrough, it seems that Xerox was not comfortable investing resources in a tool whose future application and success could not confidently be assured. Having completed their project only to see it shelved by its sponsor, Warnock and Geschke left PARC in 1982 to form their own company with the aim of further developing their code. They named their start-up venture Adobe Systems, after Palo Alto's Adobe Creek, and began working on a second-generation page-description language, which they named PostScript.

Apple

In 1979, Apple, a successful young company in which Xerox

had been among the first to invest, was developing its Lisa computer, the second commercial machine to utilise a Graphical User Interface[19]. Both Xerox and Apple knew that success lay in being able to precisely render an image visible on-screen on to a printed page without being confined to just one printer, despite Xerox having in Interpress this very ability in development. Apple's founding executive, the late Steve Jobs, had in the Lisa a product that he knew could change the world of office communications; however, poor sales of the computer did not vindicate this perspective. While Apple's rendition of the Graphical User Interface was a revelation in the world of green-on-black ASCII display text, it was to be the Lisa's successor, the seminal Macintosh, that would ultimately change that world. Seybold, who was keenly aware of the GUI progress Apple was making, realised the possibilities of a fusion with PostScript, and in 1983 he introduced Jobs to Warnock and Geschke.

Apple at this time had begun work on developing the Laser-Writer – its own version of the laser printer – in partnership with Canon, the leading printer manufacturer of the time, and so the concept of incorporating accurate page-description coding into the processor of a printer, thus freeing the mainframe hardware's capacity, was a conveniently timed breakthrough. According to Geschke, Jobs is understood to have said at this meeting: "I don't need the computer. I don't need the printer. I need the software" (Pfiffner, 2003, p.34). From that moment, Adobe, whose entire business had been modelled on manufacturing PostScript-enabled output devices, ceased to be a hardware company and became instead a software developer, producing the code by which such machines could be driven.

Raster-image processing and printing

Raster-image processing is the conversion of vector (digital) information into a high-resolution, pixelated ('raster') image.

A raster-image processor, or RIP, whether a software or firmware component, is able to interpret vector data, such as a PostScript file, as an input language, transforming it into a single bitmapped image, or output language, ready to be printed. The principal function of a raster-image processor is to produce an image that can be output for visual inspection, either on paper (plain or photographic), on some sort of visual display, or directly to film or printing plate (Seybold, 1984, p.374). Adobe's 1984 partnership with Allied Linotype, an established and respected manufacturer of typesetting equipment and typefaces, saw the realisation of the first RIP-enabled PostScript typesetter, the Linotype Linotronic 100, and later the Linotype Linotronic 300: imagesetters, as they would become known, capable of outputting resolutions of 1,270dpi and 2,540dpi (Pfiffner, 2003, p.43). In the first of these machines, a standalone raster-image processor was incorporated to interpret PostScripted page-description data, and produce a high-resolution, continuous-tone bitmap-image film that could be chemically transferred to a lithographic printing plate – a process known as computer-to-film, or CTF, imagesetting.

Raster-image printing, or laser printing, is another innovation to come from Xerox PARC, with the first laser printer being released as part of the Xerox Star 8010 computer system in 1981[20]. Utilising a mechanism similar to that of a xerographic or photographic copier, it succeeded the daisy wheel and dot-matrix office computing standards (in which rasterised or bitmapped graphics are mechanically printed on to a substrate through an ink ribbon) as a non-impact process whereby graphics are printed a pixelated line at a time, without the paper or substrate being physically struck. This produced instantly superior results, yet it would be some years before output could be considered professional typeset quality. Capable of printing multiple fonts at hitherto unseen high resolutions, the impact laser printers had upon the office environment assured the technology of their role in the revolution to come[21].

Digital typography

While the quality of output produced using laser-printing technology was undoubtedly impressive, it was mutually understood that, without access to popular typefaces (the tools by which the typesetting machine manufacturers distinguished themselves) the Adobe-Apple partnership could not and would not succeed. Jon Seybold, who shared this understanding, again orchestrated a partnership that would prove integral to the industry's acceptance of PostScript as the common page-description language. The subsequent 1984 licensing deal between Adobe, Apple, and Allied Linotype, the latter having already agreed to work with Adobe on developing the first PostScript Lynotronic typesetter, allowed Adobe and Apple to use its Times and Helvetica font families (Pfiffner, 2003, p.40), the typographic staples of the time. This deal was remarkable, as PostScript combined with desktop publishing represented a very serious threat to traditional manufacturers, whose very existence was based on the tight control of their typefaces.

Launched in 1985, Apple's first laser printer, the LaserWriter, was aimed at the domestic and office markets and came equipped with 12 fonts: regular, bold, italic, bold italic, and, in addition to Linotype's Times and Helvetica, four styles of Courier, the font used by the IBM Selectric Typesetter (Pfiffner, 2003, p.40). This choice of type gave the LaserWriter an extremely compet-itive advantage, but in order to retain its market lead, and con-sequently make PostScript the standard PDL, more fonts and PostScript-enabled devices were needed.

Adobe went on to secure a licensing deal with the International Typeface Corporation (ITC) – a significantly important distributor of typefaces in 1984 America – through which future versions of PostScript (PostScript Type 1 font format) would include ITC Bookman, ITC Avant Garde Gothic, and ITC Zapf Chancery. At the same time, and in order to further strengthen PostScript's chances of prominence as the industry standard, Adobe entered a licensing agreement with QMS, an already well-established US laser printer manufacturer.

The Apple Macintosh and LaserWriter

The Apple Macintosh computer was launched in January 1984, a year before the aforementioned LaserWriter, by a high-profile marketing campaign that deployed an advert directed by Ridley Scott and a national premiere during the half-time break of that year's Superbowl. The first commercially available (and reasonably priced[22]) desktop computer with a GUI and mouse, its acknowledged potential amidst the design and graphical arts communities was profound, yet, again, this did not immediately translate into high sales.

While the GUI and graphics handling of the Macintosh were clearly impressive, the quality of its output of images to paper was not considered professional enough by the industry: further development of PostScript was required so that the language could become truly resolution independent. For the combined Macintosh and LaserWriter – its yet-to-be-launched companion printer – to succeed, PostScript had to work flawlessly at 300dpi as well as 1,200dpi (Pfiffner, 2003, p.37), the manufacturing-standard print resolution. Adobe tweaked its code to allow for the minute scaling of characters' stem widths so that, regardless of whether content was printed through a laser printer or an industrial typesetting machine, the output would be rendered identically.

The original LaserWriter printer was powered by the industry-standard Canon LBP-CX engine and contained an Adobe-developed, PostScript-enabled processor that freed the Macintosh's limited 128kb RAM to focus on running its memory-hungry GUI software[23]. It was formally introduced in January 1985 as an addition to – and an integral part of – The Macintosh

Office[24], the concept lauded a year previously as 'freeing office workers from the drudgery of document production' (Pfiffner, 2003, p.37). With the Mac's GUI and near-typeset-quality LaserWriter printer incorporating, amongst other font families, key professional Linotype typefaces, Apple was still not achieving the high sales forecasted a year previously: The Macintosh Office had not yet been embraced by designers and office workers alike, as had been expected. Just as Adobe and Apple technologies had converged at the right time a couple of years previously, another symbiotic partnership was necessary for The Macintosh Office and desktop publishing to succeed.

What You See Is What You Get

Jon Seybold had, by 1985, published widely on the potential ground-breaking possibilities raised by the convergence of PostScript, Linotype, and Apple's Macintosh and LaserWriter. He too was surprised at the apparent market failure following The Macintosh Office launch, but he realised that the missing ingredient was a software application that would make full use of the Mac's GUI abilities.

Paul Brainerd was known to Seybold from his time working at Atex, a company in Massachusetts responsible for computerising many stages of newspaper production[25]; with former Atex colleagues he had in 1984 formed the Aldus Corporation and begun work on a PC-based, publishing-solutions software programme called PageMaker.

A hitherto inexistent concept, PageMaker was part word processor, part graphics manipulator, allowing the user to arrange both text and graphics on-screen in page-layout format. Potentially, by incorporating PageMaker into The Macintosh Office workflow, one could, for the first time, design a complete page on-screen using multiple selections of type and fonts and, with a laser printer, produce an exact rendition of this layout at near-typeset quality. This electronic process promised to replace the standard practice of mechanically splicing and pasting text, headlines, and images on to a 'paste-up' board prior to photographing. Having witnessed first-hand the programme's performance, Seybold urged Bainerd to meet with Apple and, ultimately, to switch his end-user focus from PC to Mac.

In July 1985 PageMaker was released as an application for the Macintosh, the Apple-Aldus partnership was formed, and desktop publishing as a concept was born (Pfiffner, 2003, p.54)[26]. 'WYSIWYG' (What You See is What You Get) is a term used ever since to describe this fundamental attribute of desktop publishing, and it inspired the subsequent development of many such applications to be used primarily in conjunction with the Apple Macintosh and LaserWriter.

In 1987, Adobe released its Illustrator software, which included a 'Pen' tool allowing the user to draw Bézier curves on-screen, then scale drawn objects into myriad shapes and sizes (Pfiffner, 2003, p.83)[27]. While this won the instant approval and acceptance of the design communities, it encouraged healthy competition in the form of CorelDraw and FreeHand, Aldus' accompanying application to PageMaker.

In the same year, the Colorado-based Quark company released its QuarkXPress page-layout software that, importantly, included colour-manipulation components and was considered by its users to be comparatively stable. Within three years, by version 3.0, it had become the designer's programme of choice.

Adobe's next product, PhotoShop, released in 1989, was again designed for the graphic arts market, and it would prove to be even more popular than Illustrator[28]. While Illustrator is based on PostScripted Bézier curves, allowing designers to draw line art from scratch, PhotoShop enables the manipulation of raster pixels: images taken from other sources, such as scanned artwork (Pfiffner, 2003, p.117). As the processing power of computers increased, PhotoShop became capable of producing output equivalent to that of high-performance workstations (Pfiffner, 2003, p.125), and, in conjunction with QuarkXPress and the Macintosh, it became (and remains) the *de facto* publishing design tool.

When Adobe acquired Aldus in 1994, PageMaker, which had lost almost all its share of the professional market to Quark, was redeveloped and, in 1999, was successfully rebranded as InDesign, an instantly popular competitor that, due to a superior library of Adobe digital fonts and a more user-friendly front end, soon usurped Quark's stronghold and confirmed Adobe's dominance of the desktop-publishing applications market.

The font wars

While Adobe published the specification of its PostScript PDL 'Type 3' font format in 1984, making it freely available to laser-printer manufacturers, it kept secret the specification of the 'Type 1' font format[29] (which utilised character hinting, essentially instructions to the RIP contained within the font outlines regarding which features ought to be maintained, depending on the desired output).

Consumer demand to be able to see PostScript 'Type 1' fonts on-screen brought about the release of Adobe Display Post-Script, for which a high licensing fee was sought by Adobe[30]. This close-guarded licensing monopoly created intense competition within the industry to crack the 'Type 1' specification, and led to the awkward partnering of Apple and Microsoft that resulted in TrueType, an alternative font language that could display on-screen – as well as in print – outline fonts on either a PostScript- or non-PostScript-enabled printer (Shimada, 2006). With a TrueType rasteriser built into the computer's hardware, TrueType fonts could be rasterised before they were sent to the PostScript interpreter, and rendered on-screen without the use of any third-party software[31].

In response to this strategic offensive, Adobe finally published the specifications of its 'Type 1' font format in 1990, making it freely available to anyone wishing to manufacture a PostScript printer, and announced as its successor a product called Adobe Type Manager (ATM) (Shimada, 2006). A system capable of generating on-screen PostScript display graphics[32], ATM theoretically rendered unnecessary the principals of TrueType as an alternative font technology, since Apple and Microsoft users could simply buy the software directly from Adobe, as part of its now formidable range of design applications[33].

The portable document and direct-to-plate printing

In 1993 Adobe released its most definitive product, Acrobat, a consolidated suite of software applications, including Illustrator, PhotoShop, and Acrobat Reader; programmes to be used for creating and viewing WYSIWYG documents. pdf, or Portable Document Format, derived from the fundamental principles of PostScript, is 'a file format for representing documents in a manner independent of the application software, hardware, and operating system used to create them and of the output device on which they are to be displayed or printed' (Adobe, 2001, p.33).

When computer-to-plate (CTP) and direct-to-plate (DTP) technologies succeeded those of computer-to-film (CTF) image-setting in 1994, Adobe's pdf, which was initially developed, like PostScript, for the office environment, quickly became the industry's standard prepress proofing and print medium. Using existing laser-printing techniques, platesetters enabled the digital etching of lithographic printing plates directly from a WYSIWYG application, such as pdf, eliminating the use of film and its hazardous materials and wastes, and further reducing the commitment of prepress labour, cost, and time.

By the time computer-driven platesetting, the present-day lithographic prepress standard, replaced computer-to-film image-setting, the desktop-publishing revolution had been in motion for little over a decade, yet this momentum would continue to drive and direct digital innovation in publishing and beyond. During these first years, the entire industrial prepress process changed in ways inconceivable ten years previously, when Michael Black concluded his history of Cambridge University Press by predicting – with some considered ambiguity – radical change ahead (1984, p.315). Not only had the effort of preparing copy for print been reduced, and with it the high prepress and 'makeready' costs of manufacturing, but, crucially, authorial content was reaching the publisher in digital form. No longer did the publishing process require a copy medium other than digital files, and such technical flexibility brought the control of composition under the editorial remit for the first time. As creative type design experienced a digital rebirth, text designers took a hands-on role in composition (Eliot and Rose, 2007, p.393; Hendel, 1998, pp.189–90), repurposing the traditional compositors' functions to 'DTP'-based prepress activities. It was now implicitly understood that the dominant requirement for any text processing was 'the need for flexible reuse and electronic distribution' (Eliot and Rose, 2007, p.393): the printed book had by 1994 become a by-product of the publishing process.

In order to understand how the relatively rapid introduction of these technologies revolutionised the production of Academic Books and its content at Cambridge University Press, and how these changes affected the design, typesetting and prepress man-ufacturing activities of the period, we need to be aware of the sequence in – and the means by which – they were adopted. To this end, we shall begin by considering the production processes at the Press and its Printing House in the advent of computer-led page description and design.

3

Pre-revolution book production at Cambridge

Computer-aided phototypesetting, or 'cold type', in contrast to its hot-metal predecessor, employs a process whereby light is projected, through a film-negative image of a single character in a font, on to a positive film, to produce a proofing medium known as a 'galley'[34]. The machine operator would type a proprietor-specific, binary code into a terminal computer, while a colleague would manually key the copy-edited copy, instructing the photo mechanical setting of text. Lenses were used to increase or decrease the size of type, of which there were generally a very limited number of fonts, and it would be fed into the machine on strips or disks. Changing fonts, let alone typefaces, was a laborious process[35] and, due to limited text-storage capabilities, the operators could not see the text they were typing, so each line would be keyed twice to ensure perfection. It was only when the galley film was developed on to bromide paper that the copy could be proof-read. Corrections to the galleys would be made by physically cutting characters and words from the bromide paper using precision blades and 'pasting in' replacement text, which would have to be regenerated by the same process. Once proof-read, the columns of galley text would be positioned, alongside any images, on to a paste-up board, which would be photographed in preparation of the printing plate. Compositors Paul Kahn and Krzysztof Lenk recall the effort involved in setting text by this method (1995, p.3):

Calculating the number of characters to the line was complex. Character widths varied for each font and size, as did the size of word spaces and the space between characters in a word. Before ending a line, decisions had to me made about whether and where to hyphenate the last word.

The process of Computer Aided Composition, or CAC, and the generic encoding of text was introduced to the Press in 1980 and endured a gradual phasing-in period alongside the existing letterpress technology. The initial system was designed by the University Computer Laboratory, and its unique coding was developed in-house by a man named Neil Wiseman, who became the first computer programmer to be employed by the Printing House (App. C, p.76). The hardware of this early system occupied a vast amount of space, its bank of mainframes, tape and disk drives lining entire walls of the factory floor, while its large operating terminals, with green-on-black Vector General cathode screens and 'tracker ball' cursor navigation, were manned by retrained compositors and specially recruited keyboarders.

Coinciding with this, and in support of the existing Linotron filmsetters, the Printing Division of Cambridge University Press introduced the Monotype Lasercomp imagesetter, the first device of its kind to utilise raster-image processing[36]. Initial keyboarding was performed on Coltec keyboards by eight operators capable of entering up to 9,000 characters an hour (Archive B)[37]. Regular archiving of the keyed data occurred throughout the process, beginning with the original, keyed copy being transferred to a back-up directory situated in the Nova 1 computer hard drive. From there, the copy would be manipulated on-screen, applying justification and other generic makeup parameters in preparation of the first proof, before being saved to the second hard-disk drive, Nova 2 (Archive C).

Proofs prepared using the Lasercomp imagesetter had to undergo a further language conversion, via Nova 3, producing a file format ready for laser printing, while content to be proofed using the filmsetter could come directly from the Nova 2 archive. Once proof-read on xeroxed paper copy by the Printing House readers, corrections were taken in and replacement lines of the galley text keyed by the Coltec keyboard operators. Another archive copy was made and stored on Nova 2, as before, and the procedure was repeated with the corrected first-proof data being output to film or bromide (Archive A)[38]. Once assembled into pages of typeset text by the Paper Makeup department, paper copies of this final page proof were delivered to the customer and then returned with annotations, which would require further rekeying and a repeat of the aforementioned archiving process. Once approved as 'final', the content would once again pass through Paper Makeup, resulting in camera-ready copy that could be passed to the Pre-press department for impositioning and, finally, made ready for press.

Computer-aided photocomposition at the Press evolved over the years through several updates of its hardware and software so that, by the end of the 1980s, it was established as the main typesetting service offered by the Printing House[39]. Traditionally, this service was designed not for the Publishing Division but for external customers, in response to demand and at a consequentially high price. Cambridge Printing had always been a 'high end' typesetter and printer, and it held a client base that consisted of major publishers (such as Addison Wesley, Blackwell, Chambers, Chapman & Hall, Elsevier, Hodder & Stoughton, Routledge, and Taylor & Francis), and maintained a comparatively limited relationship with the CUP Publishing Division, specifically Academic Books (App. B, p.69). With this high-quality service came high costs, which meant that the majority of Academic Book titles, though always printed on-site at Cambridge, were mostly typeset elsewhere. Depending on the product being created and, if it were part of a series, its associated style and formatting rules, a multitude of external typesetting vendors were employed (including Bath Press, Paxton Press in Suffolk, Wyvern Typesetting in Bristol, Servis Filmsetting and Vision Typesetting in Manchester, and, occasionally, Graphicraft, a specialist typesetter in Hong

Kong[40]). Aside from the consideration of cost in relation to the predicted profitability of a product, the choice of typesetters, each of whom employed their own phototypesetting system and associated proprietary typefaces, was determined by the type of work that they could typically take on.

The pre-revolution book-production process

Design

When a manuscript entered Production, following successful proposal, review, and syndication, it would be assessed by a production controller, whose knowledge of the available printing and typesetting processes would enable him or her to choose a typesetter from a range of suppliers (App. E, p.127). For instance, a book belonging to a series might automatically be assigned a typesetter, and the job booked in, based on the setter's established history of producing similar titles[41].

For books not adhering to a specified series, a bespoke design specification would be created post-copy-editing, and the appointment of a suitable supplier would be made as a consequence of its assigned layout and style[42]. For bespoke designs, the manuscript would be sent to a copy-editor and returned to Production some weeks later, during which time a second copy of the manuscript would enter what was known as the 'preliminary design stage', from which an accurate 'cast-off' based on the final word count could be determined[43]. The text designer would produce a layout, drawn by hand on sheets of A3 paper, defining the marginal spaces (including back, side, foredge and foot measurements) and the interior, printed spaces (including the font, type depth and width) (App. E, p.127).

This preliminary bespoke specification, together with a sampled composite layout and the original manuscript, would be sent to a selection of suppliers for quotation, to ultimately determine which typesetter would be employed, and from this a cast-off could be obtained, enabling the production controller to forecast the production's typesetting cost. When the copy-edited manuscript – bearing generic markup codes in its margins in addition to stylistic amendments to the text – returned to Production, it entered its 'final design stage', in which the book's preliminary pages (i.e. the front matter) were specified, and stylistic rulings (such as headings, quotations, tables, lists, footnotes, references, etc.) assigned to each coded text element.

It was at this stage that a book's artwork, which had accompanied the manuscript through copy-editing in the form of 'roughs', would be prepared, a task that the in-house text designer would commission from the Printing Division's Drawing Office, as well as from a small pool of freelance illustrators (App. E, p.130). The rough-artwork material included annotations made by the copy-editor, among them concise labelling and numbering details, and other stylistic instructions from the text designer relating to the specification. Once received, the redrawn artwork would be sent to the copy-editor, who would obtain approval from the author, a process that could involve several returns to the illustrator via Production before completion[44].

Typesetting

Once finalised, the artwork and the coded, edited manuscript were ready for typesetting and they were sent out to the relevant pre-appointed vendor with a brief to produce galley proofs showing only text as it would appear according to the design specification. Once they had been printed to either bromide 'galley' paper (in cases of complicated, double-column layouts), or xeroxed pages taken from the bromide (for the typical monographs or series books), the typesetter would deliver to the production controller, via Design, a series of unpaginated proofs bearing printer trim markings[45]. Typically, typesetting page rates did not allow for any changes to be made once the proofs had been set, and so scales were put in place to govern any subsequent revision, be it from the publisher or author. Before despatching the proofs, the typesetter would perform their own checks on the output, indicating in green pen instances of error produced by the keyboarding of the manuscript's content[46]. Red pen would be used by the author, or the proof-reader employed by the publisher, to indicate typesetting errors not disclosed by the earlier typesetter's checks. Blue ink was used by the author and publisher to denote any additional changes that were chargeable to the publisher, and both the author's and reader's annotated proofs would return to Production to be collated together by the copy-editor, producing one master, annotated proof (App. E, p.133). This master would then be seen by the in-house text designer who, using the relevant specification or pattern copy and the original, marked-up manuscript as references, would check each typeset element, a process that could take several days to complete, before returning it to the typesetter. There followed, as there does today, a subsequent proofing round, where the annotated master first proof was compared in-house, page for page, against the typesetter's revised interpretation, and, depending on the typesetting system, electronic archives made from its copy. Occasionally this process of revision was repeated until the text was approved by the publisher as ready for press and the camera-ready copy could be ordered.

Prepress

On receipt of its camera-ready copy, which arrived at the Printing House in boxes of bromide sheets, a job would be processed by the Paper Makeup department and impositioned by the Pre-press department according to the signature format defined by the printing press to be used. The process of imposition, whereby eight, sixteen, or thirty-two pages could be photographed to produce a sheet of film from which a photomechanical printing plate could be developed, was a laboured process, involving three people at any one time: one to operate the camera, photographing images; another working in the dark room, developing film; and a third processing the film, in preparation of final proofs and for the next stage, platemaking (App. D, p.89). Each shift would typically involve ten people working on light tables, imposing the single-page films into signature film, from which proofs were produced and approved before the printing plate was developed (App. D, p.89)[47].

For single-colour, text-only work, the bromide sheets were positioned on a board according to a predetermined sequence (which accounted for the eventual folding of the sheet when printed), and then photographed to film, from which the resulting printing plates were exposed by UV light in a vacuum-sealed plate frame, ensuring tight contact between film and plate (App. D, p.89). Any line-drawn, illustrative material would be received separately to the text bromides, and manually positioned alongside the text on the board, prior to being photographed.

For colour-film processing, such as a full-colour, continuous-tone photograph or coloured text, each component colour was manually separated by applying red, green, and blue filters to a master film, exposing a separate film for each, from which an individual plate would be made[48]. A fourth colour, black, was created to attain contrast by shadowing greys and other dark areas of the image. By this method of process-colour separation, a single-page colour proof took one hour to produce, and therefore two hours for every signature (App. D, p.91). An average ten-signature proofing job would take a prepress technician twenty hours of undivided attention to complete[49].

When, in 1996, automated computer systems were finally introduced to the manufacturing end of Printing's operations, the design, copy-editing and prepress stages of a typical book's production were performed entirely by hand, a process that had remained unchanged through successive generations of skilled craftsmen and mechanical technologies. With the arrival of

Postscript page-description and raster-image laser printing came a revolutionary change to the methods by which books were produced at Cambridge. The production process, from beginning to end, became digitised and, as a result, significant reductions in time and cost were achieved, and the value of content ownership and the pressing need for structured, reusable data were realised.

4

Post-revolution book production
at Cambridge

By the late 1980s, the majority of authorial manuscripts were being submitted to the Press on disk, and initially these disks were
discarded by the Publishing Division on receipt, the assumption
being that the existing production processes could not utilise their
content (App. C, p.78). The Technical Applications Group (TAG)
was established in 1989 as a means to capture this data as it entered the typesetting system, removing the need to rekey text, and
thus simplify the process[50]. At the time, this copy was submitted
in multiple formats – on tape and disk, and all variations thereof[51]. Employing an Intermedia disk-reading device to interpret the
content with an array of disk drives, the user applied predefined
translation tables to convert each file's WYSIWYG formatting
into the proprietary language being used in-house (App. C, p.80).
By design, this process was automated, requiring minimal intervention once the translation script had been run, and, in addition
to reducing the amount of keyboarding required, it removed the
need to manually code each keyed manuscript on-screen.

There soon followed another important introduction to the
workflow: the Interset pagination system, a WYSIWYG precursor to the arrival of desktop publishing at Cambridge (App. C,
p.70). Interset could generate whole pages of typeset text and
illustrations (as opposed to non-paginated columns of galley
text) as PostScript files and send them directly to a Lasercomp
imagesetter. Again, this fully automated pagination system delivered an immediate reduction in the time it took to produce proofs.
However, it was initially used only for one customer, The Royal
Society, which at the time had four journals being produced by
Cambridge[52]. At approximately £50 per typeset page, the Society

was understandably keen that the Printing House should adopt the technology in order to improve efficiency (App. C, p.79). The Interset system allowed the user to apply formatting rules to on-screen text 'on the fly', using a split-screen WYSIWYG/coding viewer to assess in real time the resulting changes. Used in conjunction with the Intermedia disk reader, the Interset pagination system provided Cambridge with a blueprint from which it could develop its own in-house pagination software, incorporating an updated version of the generic code that by this point had been in place for little over a decade. In 1992, at approximately the same time as the Interset system was being trialled, desktop publishing, in the form of Apple Macintosh computers and Quark page-layout software, was introduced to TAG[53]. However, it was another four years before the Prepress department became fully computer-ised, utilising WYSIWYG technologies in imposition and plate making. It was due to pressure applied by its external customers that Cambridge Printing invested in desktop publishing, employing two experienced operators to work alongside the TeX and disk-converting teams within the Technical Applications Group (App. F, p.151). By 1996 the process of producing most Cambridge titles had become entirely digital, influenced greatly by the desktop-publishing innovations from a decade before. In addition to revolutionising the way in which authors created and submitted their content, this gradual yet seismic change had revolutionised the design, typesetting, and prepress stages of production.

The post-revolution book-production process

Design and typesetting

The traditionally employed methods of text design remained, in theory, the same, but the tools and media that were used became computerised. For bespoke text designs, page layouts were created in QuarkXPress and content from the authorial Word files was used to produce sample 'composite' pages. Typesetters were still selected on their expertise and historical association with a product, but, by 1996, their prime services had shifted to desktop publishing, and, eventually, for most this would mean the end, as more and more offshore vendors emerged to offer fiercely competitive page rates. Customers were no longer prepared to be confined to any one vendor's proprietary system, and so, with future retrieval and reprocessing of their content in mind, they demanded ownership of the final print files.

At Cambridge, text designers would create a specification of each layout that, if a particularly complex design, would be converted into a template by the desktop-publishing team in TAG before being sent with a copy-edited manuscript for typesetting (App. F, p.153). For the majority of titles, the typesetting template would be generated by the supplier, based on the specification provided by Cambridge. Series designs, which already had predefined, hand-written specifications, were also translated to QuarkXPress templates by TAG, while, in 1993, design 'standards' were introduced, enabling whole categories of books to be assigned a generic style and layout, thus creating a simpler specification process for producing fewer typesetting templates (App, F, p.83).

In order to ensure consistency within the various series, the Monotype Company was commissioned in 1991 to convert the photomechanical typefaces being used by the Press' own typesetting system into PostScript fonts, which could be used by Macs running QuarkXPress[54]. Typesetting at Cambridge had historically employed a whole department of proof-readers to check all output, prior to it being delivered as a proof to a customer. Often, proofing galleys 'blind' and without a 'top' copy of the original marked-up manuscript for reference, the readers provided a service that went beyond verifying accuracy: they assessed the content as well as the format of every title produced. With the introduction of desktop publishing and the increase in demand from customers that the typesetting page rates be reduced in line with the rest of the industry, the pool of proof-readers gradually decreased in size until the service was removed altogether (App, F, p.79)[55]. Because content was now entering the typesetting system already made up and paginated, it could be checked by the operator on-screen, output to proof on paper, and sent directly to the customer for approval. For typesetting that was being done externally, typically in Quark-XPress, the final source files would be delivered to the Press and to the TAG, where they could be converted to PostScript and sent to Prepress to be imposed.

Digital 'prepress'

The Prepress department employed the services of two proof-readers, who were tasked with checking all output to proof (App. D, p.100). Single-colour text work, which constitutes the majority of Academic Book output, was, until 1998, still being processed to plate as camera-ready copy, in common with industry practice. It was only after a succession of imposition-software instalments that the Prepress department started to receive text directly from typesetters as PostScript files, despite the fact that for years content had been typeset using PostScript (App. D, p.116). The reason for this was that the early file processors were not equipped to deal with large-format sheet sizes, such as those necessary for printing thirty-two-page signatures[56], or illustration-heavy page layouts. Pages of text that included illustrations were printed to bromide paper by the typesetter and submitted for imposition, as per the traditional workflow. In fact, the first files that were processed electronically belonged to covers: smaller, two-page files that could be manipulated on-screen with comparative ease.

In 1996 the first WYSIWYG system was introduced to the Prepress department and with it a drum scanner and the Press' first imagesetter (App. D, p.117). The TaigaSPACE system was a Unix-powered production workstation designed to process high volumes of page data, created by desktop-publishing systems, in order to produce professionally 'trapped' and imposed output[57].

Paired with a Macintosh computer, the system could receive PostScript, EPS, DCS, and TIFF file formats (the latter being input directly from the drum scanner) as well as source files taken from QuarkXPress and Pagemaker applications. Importantly, it could batch-process in the background, freeing the operator to work simultaneously on multiple jobs. Covers would be submitted by the Drawing Office as source files, typically QuarkXPress, and converted to Postscript on the Prepress Macs prior to being fed into the Taiga workflow and ripped so that the image produced on-screen was an accurate representation of the final output to the imagesetter. The Taiga's WYSIWYG viewer, the first prepress editor of its kind, allowed the operator to gauge the individual colour values and separations, and also the trapping prior to committing to film and producing a final proof, a hitherto inconceivable possibility. Despite the myriad advantages that this system brought to Prepress, it was initially used for just twenty per cent of the work, the remainder still being imposed, or 'planned', by hand (App. D, p.93). In all, ten people were employed directly by the Taiga system, processing covers, scanning artwork and producing bromide proofs, with another twenty people manually imposing pages on the light tables.

In 1998, and in order to receive and process final PostScript text files, an additional software installation, called Imposition Publisher, was procured and enabled the on-screen imposition of larger-format sheets: signatures of up to thirty-two pages (App. D, p.94). As a software RIP, and in the advent of pdf (which had yet to establish itself as the standard file format for outputting PostScripted content), Imposition Publisher interpreted each incoming file by utilising different drivers, a process that required regular updating, depending on the files' origin. By the use of drivers in this way, embedded fonts did not have to be stored on the hardware RIP. However, due to this reliance on software downloads there was a problem inherent in the system: should a particular driver become outdated, corruption could occur within the text during the RIP and characters could 'drop out', the error being realised only when the file had printed to film (App. D, p.117). The proofing of this output, therefore, was integral to the assurance of prepress quality. The addition of Imposition Publisher to the prepress workflow saw the end of camera-ready copy at Cambridge as, by then, all final typeset files were received as PostScript code[58]. A second imagesetter was installed and the Opticopy and Littlejohn[59] cameras were removed, and with them the camera-operators' jobs[60]. In 1999 the first electronic proofing device, a digital chromalin machine, was installed, followed later by two Agfa Sherpa plotter machines, which enabled the operator to check a proof on-screen as well as by eye on paper, reducing the requirement for a separate proofing stage in the process and, as a consequence, saving valuable time and resources. Imposition Publisher was replaced in 2000 by another, more reliable file-processing application called Impact, which, like its successor, Prinergy, could receive and impose directly from pdf files[61], and the physical space previously occupied by the cameras was reconfigured to make room for the hardware installation of the first Lotem platesetter[62].

Advanced typesetting and back-end SGML

From the outset in 1989, the TAG employed seven operators, including programmers, dealing mainly with disk-conversion, and, due to the uptake of desktop publishing and TeX typesetting, this number had grown to twenty by the time the TAG joined the mainstream Composition department in 1996 (App. F, p.150; App. C, p.81)[63]. Always a unique, proprietary system, the Cambridge CAC process, which was devised some fifteen years previously, had never been assigned a name until, following the convergence of the two typesetting systems, CATS was introduced. The Cambridge Advanced Typesetting System (CATS) incorporated the unique Cambridge typesetting code, which applied generic markup to all processed content before running it against individual product Job Description codes to produce specified formatting. In addition, it was reconfigured in 1995 to enable SGML conversion at the end of the typesetting process, providing the customer with a second output (App. C, p.83). Again, the demand for SGML in addition to print-ready source files came initially from external customers, while, internally, it was used by the Journals Division, whose Cambridge Journals Online went live in 1996[64].

From its earliest incarnation in 1980, the typesetting system employed at Cambridge utilised a proprietary form of generic markup, which remained in practice until 2002 when composition ceased to be a service provided on-site (App. C, p.71). During this tumultuous period, the entire production process, from manuscript creation to printed book, had changed, and with it the understanding of what 'production' meant to the publisher. As an independent printer and typesetter, Cambridge Printing made changes that were wholly driven by customer demand and, consequently, the Press invested heavily in technology at a time when other onshore typesetting vendors and printers struggled to survive in an ever-shrinking domestic market. By the turn of the century, the desktop-publishing revolution, which at first promised to deliver efficiency and control to the publisher, had left its mark on a dissipated typesetting industry. Composition at Cambridge Printing, with its high-end customer base, secured a dedicated stream of investment at a time when the smaller, proprietor-based vendors could not, due to the majority of their work being better suited, both financially and technically, to external locations that provided larger-scale – and therefore more cost-effective – repetitive work. For this reason, composition at Cambridge in 1996 was well placed to continue its operations and weather the era's technological and financial storms, albeit for just another five years.

5

Conclusion

Writing in 1984, the four-hundredth year of continuous printing at CUP, and as the desktop-publishing revolution reached its tipping point in the US, the former University Publisher, Michael Black, concluded his History by saying (1984, p.315):

> *It is already obvious that the new technology of word-processing facilities interfacing with computer typesetting may, skilfully developed, counterbalance the present economic effects of recession, and be exploited in any future period of growth. Indeed in the very near future the technology of book production may become radically different in ways inconceivable to the printers of earlier times.*

The technology of book production did indeed become radically different and, over a period of thirty years, the Press' visionary aspirations for the capture and handling of content evolved at the forefront of technical innovation to become today the backbone of its publishing operations. While this achievement was due in part to the desktop-publishing revolution of the late 1980s and the implementation of generic encoding, which produced cheaper and simpler output for printing, the resulting print quality was at times threatened by technical progress. Because of this, the acceptance of a revised tolerance for the printed book's appearance has given way to a drive for creating versatile content from which the printed book has become just one output.

The realisation of the importance of generically coding content during the 'origination' stages of production had existed at Cambridge since the beginning of the 1980s, and the need

44

for multi-purposed publishing formats was understood many years before the arrival of the internet and its promise of myriad digital publishing possibilities. However, due to a mixture of financial conservatism and a non-cohesive operational structure, the Academic Books division in 1996 chose not to invest in an XML workflow (which by then had replaced SGML and its online reincarnation, HTML) as the standard meta-language structuring tool for Books, and instead remained focused on print. Following the implementation in 2005 of front-end XML workflows, and a corresponding general DTD, the Cambridge Books Online platform went live in 2010, some fourteen years after the pioneering Cambridge Journals Online (App. B, p.73).

The desktop-publishing revolution brought improvements to the time and cost with which output was generated at the Press, thus making viable the Academic Books monograph publishing strategy, and its innovative technologies established more control in the pre-press operations of Printing. However, it can be said that the general quality standard of printed output was lowered accordingly. In 2012, at the time of writing, the annual output of 975 Academic & Professional Book titles was overseen by one in-house text design manager, and the composition of bespoke specifications was outsourced to a small pool of freelance suppliers[65]. In 1989, by contrast, when QuarkXPress and page-description layout applications had yet to be embraced, a new book handed over to Production at Cambridge was assigned to one of seven text designers working exclusively for the Academic Books Division, which at the time was producing 444 tiles a year[66]. Each title that passed through the copy-editing process did so under the supervision of a professional designer, so that the job, when submitted to a typesetter, was in compliance with the centuries-old Cambridge quality standard. While the quality of books output today is still of a relatively high standard, the actual standard itself has been compromised by the automation and openness afforded by desktop publishing. The introduction

45

of computer-drawn design templates and standard text designs has meant that the majority of Academic titles no longer require a final design stage. It also means that, for the most part, the preliminary design stage is no longer the vital process that it had been in determining a typesetting workflow and securing a cast-off. People without a formal training in book design were given access to a once reverentially segregated aspect of production, and consequently they influenced the manner in which style was utilised within the Cambridge brand. This amateurish input, coupled with an increasing ownership of content by the Editorial and Marketing departments, caused in some cases a withdrawal of typographic values from the printed page – removing from the designer the ownership of aesthetic control.

External customers began to deliver page-formatted PageMaker and QuarkXPress files for typesetting at Cambridge, resulting in extensive delays while the TAG reprocessed the content to make it suitable for printing[67]. With decreasing numbers of onshore vendors providing increasingly specific typesetting services, the bulk of Academic LaTeX and some book composition started to move to offshore suppliers in 1994. Almost ten years later, by 2003, typesetting had all but gone from Cambridge Printing, and the TAG was decommissioned and replaced by Content Services. The focus had shifted from composition using proprietary coding to validating source files received from external typesetting suppliers and preparing these for printing on- and off-site. Aside from the savings made in typesetting page costs, the time and efficiency with which page proofs were generated – and therefore books produced – was greatly improved. However, due to the automation of the various page-description programmes being used, a relaxation occurred in age-old composition rules concerning hyphenation and line and page endings in order to process the final files received. Additionally, the standardisation of the content being supplied was inconsistent. Source files taken, typically, from Quark-XPress often contained non-proprietary 'workarounds', shortcut coding implemented on an ad-hoc basis by various vendors without disclosing their significance to file integrity (App. A, p.56). Such variances went unnoticed at the time of receipt and proved problematic only when a file was selected for reuse, by which point the problem was irreversible. In order to deal with this data-validation issue, the Asset Store was established in 1998 as a pioneering content-management system into which typesetting source files, as well as corresponding pdf print files, were stored. While this solved the problem of reuse, ultimately in the form of reprinting, the source code remained in many cases unstandardised.

The Asset Store was replaced in 2011 by the Cambridge Asset Management System (CAMS), which, in addition to receiving, validating and archiving multiple end 'deliverables' (including final 'CBML', the Cambridge Books Online source code) provides a global infrastructure through which all areas of the Press conduct business. Today, the XML-encryption of all Academic & Professional Book content (including monographs, textbooks and coursebooks, trade crossovers, as well as whole lists of professional learning material) is initiated at the beginning of production, providing versatile online marketing material many months ahead of publication. In addition to the final print pdf file, the resulting outputs consist of ePub files, for content delivered to iOS platforms, mobi files for those of the Amazon Kindle, 'smart' pdf files for repositories and generic electronic reading devices, as well as XML and CBML-translated data for the Cambridge Books Online platform. On receipt from suppliers of the final XML source code, the print pdf is validated by the Content Services department before being sent to one of several printers around the world, depending on the markets to which the print run is designated. During the time it takes to print, bind and distribute the physical book stock, the other outputs are generated via external suppliers and validated in-house, enabling simultaneous global publication.

While the printed book, regardless of where its pdf is printed, will retain its structural and typographic integrity, the content that is viewed on an iPad will not be entirely consistent with that shown on a Kindle or Android device. The acceptance of a revised tolerance to the overall standard with which printed output is generated has led to new concerns regarding both existing content platforms and those that have yet to take a market share. Over a period of thirty years, the printed book has changed in response to the innovation of desktop-publishing technologies, yet the resulting era of digital content dissemination remains in its infancy. To echo the words of Michael Black when concluding his history of Cambridge publishing in 1984, the future of Cambridge Academic Books content production and delivery, while already well provisioned, now depends on the further evolution and standardisation of digital platforms, which, when achieved, will ensure consistency of quality across all outputs.

Long live the book, in whatever form that may be.

Acknowledgements

I wish to thank my dissertation supervisor, Dr Nancy Roberts, whose encouragement and advice at all times motivated and inspired me. I am also wholly indebted to the six interviewees who each gave up very generous amounts of time to talk with me and relive the past: Michael Holdsworth, Pauline Ireland, Chris Mckeown, Noel Robson, Stephanie Thelwell, and Brenda Youngman. In addition to the interviews that were recorded, many emails and words were exchanged between us in the weeks and months that followed. It is for this additional help and willingness to assist that I am especially grateful. Other thanks are due to Dr Rosalind Grooms, the Press archivist at The University Library, for her introduction to the archive and for helping me trawl through it; to Graham Hart and Chris McLeod, of Hart McLeod Ltd., whose bursary in 2009 allowed me to enrol on the MA course; to Dr Sam Rayner and Dr Leah Tether, of Anglia Ruskin University, for their counsel and support; and to my senior colleagues at the Press, Richard Fisher and Kevin Taylor, for their practical help in retrieving data from various Press databases. Damian Penfold, with whom I once worked on a project whereby CBML code was set in a letterpress brace, kindly granted permission to use the photo used in the volume's cover artwork and frontispiece. Finally, I wish to thank my Press mentor and friend, the late Dr Alison Mander, for the self-belief she instilled in me while I worked as part of her production department.

Oral histories

The transcripts of the oral histories recorded as part of the research provide an important historical and contextual record of this period of publishing history. The following appendices, which are indexed on pages 174–180, contain verbatim accounts of the conversations that took place in early 2012[68].

Appendix A: Transcript of interview with Michael Holdsworth

Michael Holdsworth began his career at the Press in 1983, having previously worked at Allen & Unwin, and took on the dual role of Publishing Operations Director and Social Sciences Group Director. He introduced the first Macintosh computers to the Publishing Division and unified the Press' information systems as a primary focus. As Press Business Development Director, he later concentrated on new technology issues: initiatives for content and rights management, production workflows, print on demand (POD), and electronic publishing developments.

Appendix B: Transcript of interview with Pauline Ireland

Pauline Ireland joined the Press in Cambridge as a publishing assistant in the Journals department in January 1985 and moved into Journals production work, becoming a production controller in 1987. She left Journals to take over as Production and Design Manager of the STM (book) group in 1989 and remained there until January 1994, when she moved to New York to assume the role of Production Manager for the North American Branch. She subsequently became Director of Production and New Media, and in 2006 she took on the new role of Special Projects Director.

Appendix C: Transcript of interview with Chris Mckeown

Chris Mckeown began his Press career in 1978 as an apprentice hot-metal compositor before the introduction of phototypesetting, when he became a programmer of the Press' unique Computer Aided Composition language. He was the manager of the Technical Applications Group and the mainstream Composition department, before becoming Director of Composition when the two groups merged. He went on to be the Journals Production Director before leaving in 2003 to work for the typesetter, Aptara Inc., formerly Techbooks.

Appendix D: Transcript of interview with Noel Robson

Noel Robson joined the Press in 1992 in the Printing House camera room as one of two prepress apprentices, the first in more than ten years, studying on block release at the Cambridge School of Art. In 2006 he became the Printing Division's Reprographics Supervisor, responsible for the entire 'prepress' print operation. He is currently the Creative and Technical Lead for Academic Books.

Appendix E: Transcript of interview with Stephanie Thelwell

Stephanie Thelwell began her career at the Press in 1989 as a Book Designer for the Science Group, having previously worked as a designer and medical illustrator for the National Health Service. A talented artist, she is currently the Design Manager for Academic Books.

Appendix F: Transcript of interview with Brenda Youngman

Brenda Youngman joined the Press in 1992 as the first desktop publishing typesetter in the Technical Applications Group (TAG), having previously worked with Macintosh page-layout applications in the States. She is currently a Senior Content Distribution Controller within the Content Services department.

Appendix A

Transcript of interview with Michael Holdsworth
Wednesday, 25th January 2012
Michael Holdsworth's home, Cambridge, 16.00pm

On arriving at the Press in 1983...

I was always combining editorial and book acquisition with operations. Basically, I ran what was then the Social Sciences Group. At that point Social Sciences was separate from Humanities and was much bigger because it had History in it, for some strange reason. It was the largest publishing group. I ran my personal publishing with a series of good, young editorial assistants. Richard Fisher was the principal one of those. When I came to the Press in 1983, I combined being a Group Director with being Publishing Operations Director. I was reforming things and changing things, but doing it very much from the inside. In a way, it was much easier to make these changes because whenever I introduced something challenging or unpopular, I could say "Well, I'm doing this myself too and all my editors are doing it, and that's how it's going to be".

That's quite a unique position to have had. Was that the agreement when you were taken on?

Yes. And it was unique. All the way through to the late '90s, I had authors and was publishing books. You could write an interesting history about how the introduction of personal computers, desktop machines, transformed the way all the marketing and production were done, all the way down to spreadsheets, forms, Syndicate papers, and scheduling – things like that. And there's also how the changes were made to doing books. The actual changes to doing books were not associated with the first desktop computers much. Equally, it has a long history: filmsetting, which was computerised, was going on in the late 1970s and, in the very early '80s, there were PCs in use and programmes – these were all pre-Windows – there was word processing with things like WordPerfect and pre-Microsoft, pre-Windows, applications. And there were spreadsheet programmes; things like VisiCalc. Much more in New York than in Cambridge.

There were certainly, in the very early '80s, editors, one in particular, who used to strap a large mini-computer on to a luggage trolley and take it home on weekends! This was before Macintosh [and] the whole business of how easy it became to do things. I think the trick at Cambridge, in terms of getting people to commit to change, was all about Macintosh. From about 1984, we had an entire workforce that had never picked up a mouse, that was faced with word processing on a PC, which was DOS, pre-Windows. No Graphical User Interface at all on-screen: it was all green screens and boxes. If you wanted to change a font in to italic in WordPerfect, you had to use a series of keystrokes. But the Macintosh enabled you to do all that stuff. We got a very reluctant workforce up to speed quite quickly on what were always, right from the very beginning, shared machines with shared learning. This may sound like decades ago, but it wasn't that long ago. And, of course, where we started was with a public personal computer. The Press was very, very conservative.

What I'm trying to say is that is was really hard and expensive to move from the one computer that everybody had to book on to – booking by the hour almost – to everybody having one. But even so, all that was happening at Cambridge years before anywhere else. It was clear to me that, at the editorial and production level you wanted to be in a position where, ideally, you would enter all the data once, and it would be used for marketing, production scheduling, forms for producing Syndicate papers, contracts, etc. by using basic databases. And we had in Filemaker a miraculous thing that enabled you to incorporate special sorts, bold and italics, things that were hard to do in other programmes of the time. It was very user-friendly and obvious. So many of the general staff of the Press, whether they were in their twenties, thirties, or forties, had never seen a computer until they saw a Macintosh and they just went straight in to it. That's what we did – an editorial group working with me, integrating marketing and production with the concept of the price-working to see how books would work or not financially.

How did that happen, prior to this point?

What happened before was that was a VisiCalc-type programme: a standalone application running on an ICL machine. At that point there was a distributed computing system within the Press at the office level called DRS, a branch of ICL, but most people did their price-workings on the back of an envelope. There was no Excel. In fact, when we did the price-working, we didn't actually do it in a spreadsheet programme at all, we simply built it from the ground up in Filemaker.

Of course, Filemaker is still prevalent now, both in Editorial and Production.

Is it still there? That's just amazing. As I've said so many times, if anybody had any idea that we were writing systems that would still be used twenty, thirty years later… I suppose it's probably because there hasn't been anybody who really wanted to change it. Even the famous Asset Store… I can remember vividly, in about 1998, one of the potential partners we were talking to about how we might do it, saying 'We might use as a standardised format this thing that Adobe's developing called pdf. Have you heard of it?' I said 'Yes, I've heard of pdf. It looks quite interesting but it's very proprietary and I'm not sure if it's going to catch on'. And then there was great discussion that pdf was probably going to be adopted by the American military as a document standard.

Was anybody going to want to put their documents in to a format basically owned by Adobe? We decided to go with pdf as the standard for the Asset Store, regardless of typesetting source files, which obviously would be held separately by typesetters. We decided to have a pdf version of everything as well. I thought the Asset Store would last five years.

Surely it has turned out to be a good decision?

I don't know. It was very expensive. In a way, so many of these things have stopped better solutions being implemented. Dear old Asset Store...

My supervisor, Nancy Roberts, was telling me that just last week she met with her counterparts at OUP, who are interested in the present Cambridge asset management system (CAMS), and was shocked to discover that their historical content was being stored here and there on CD ROMs.

There have been one or two other really big asset store implementations. Wiley was doing a huge one. I used to give loads of talks on this subject and had a wonderful slide from HarperCollins showing a rack of CDs which someone has labelled 'not ABBA'. They were obviously in ABBA CD cases. There is another photograph – again, HarperCollins – of a luggage trunk containing CDs and, written across it in felt tip is 'Ask Angela for the key'. The idea of having digital assets on CD in a box on-site!

Would you say that the Cambridge decision to invest in an asset store at that time was ahead of the industry?

I don't think there's any question. It was way ahead of its time. You've got to bear in mind that at that point there were no proprietary solutions. Content-management systems nowadays are packages that sit behind websites, a way for people to load text, photographs and pricing information, and database content to manage a website, such as the system used to manage Amazon. That's not what we were talking about. There were some document-management systems around, but again they were incredibly primitive. They didn't have the kind of flexibility we were trying to build into the Asset Store in terms of what sorts of objects it could hold, and so on. The whole idea of storing something once, properly, labelling it properly, making sure it was complete... There were nightmare scenarios, from which one was trying to get away from, that were absolutely rife. Typesetters would go out of business and you'd lose everything. Typesetters were working in Quark, or 3B2 – whatever system it was and particularly, the Indians were terrible at this – they'd be writing mini-programmes. You'd find that some Welsh cooperative were doing cottage-industry typesetting, and one of them had written some rogue workaround to a problem in Quark, which they'd all used, or an Indian typesetter had modified Word to do something particular. Nobody else could read or repurpose these typesetting files. Even though they were supposedly written in proprietary format, they weren't. They were non-standardised. New editions, for instance, were a nightmare because you only discovered when you went to use the typesetter or printer files that Chapter Five was missing, or that everything was incorrectly labelled. There'd be no conversion control.

The other thing that used to happen in film, especially in pre-lims, was that people used to get the scissors or scalpel out, so you'd have a situation where someone would notice a mistake in the film at some proofing stage and they'd go to another piece of film that they weren't using and cut out an Icelandic character, or the rule that was the right thickness, and stick it in to make it work and make the plates. The plates weren't kept but the film was, so you'd have one piece of film that matched the origination and another piece of film with pieces chopped out of it. The Printing House was dreadful at this. The whole business of film was that you had to produce a camera-ready image that was 'okay'. If you were changing prelims for new editions, just get the knife out! So, it was a case of having things correctly named and knowing that they were backed up in a consistent format.

Who led that decision, the realisation of the importance of doing this?

It was entirely me. This was 1999–2000, maybe a bit later. I was always excited about innovation and change, doing things differently. It was a real struggle. A struggle to get the funding for the Asset Store.

I can imagine that getting people on side for that would have been quite tricky.

Yes. And you've got these cosy relationships that still exist between Production and suppliers, and of course we had all the issues with the Printing Division when it was doing its own origination. Basically what happened with typesetting and origination is that there was a long period when the Printing Division thought that it could reinvent typesetting software and improve on typesetting engines like 3B2 or Quark. And they did develop CATS, but it seemed a crazy thing, to me, to do. I used to quote them as saying 'We don't think Microsoft Word is good enough for our word processing so we will write our own'. It was a ludicrous thing to be doing but that did happen and that was used for what they could control the use of it for, which was basically the typesetting of Cambridge Journals, long after all the typesetting for Cambridge Books was being done elsewhere.

So just journals were typeset using the proprietary system?

Yes. My memory of all that stuff is blurred, to be honest. It was just happening. It developed in to a whole system, which was then tied up when the Printing Division made an agreement with SR Nova in Bangalore, a tied relationship whereby they would only typeset using the Cambridge system. I guess that was about ten years ago.

This wasn't the beginning of the offshore relationships?

No, that was the first offshore relationship, but that was a Journals relationship. The start of the [Books] offshore relationships involved finding new typesetters, I don't know who the main suppliers are now?

Aptara (Techbooks), Newgen, SPi and Integra.

Those were the basic four that we started with. Techbooks is a strange story. It was a small, second-generation Indian-American company. The founders of Techbooks were three siblings, two brothers and a sister, who would only be in their fifties now – so very young then – who set up doing TeX typesetting, when TeX started to explode as a mathematical and science typesetting programme. Extraordinarily interestingly, they, as a part-American company were doing this with graduate students in America in a genuine desktop publishing type of way for lots of American science publishers, because of their extraordinary expertise with TeX. They were also tied up in Delhi with a business they bought there as a little grunt-work outsourcing business. So, they were an American business with people who would consider themselves to be American and built this massive new business in India. When we started looking for new typesetters, all those businesses were outfits where I made the initial contact. SR Nova carried on doing Journals for the Printing Division and we were basically looking for Indian typesetters to work for Publishing. At that time, we weren't particularly fussed whether they'd be following our new XML rules. That came later. All we cared about initially was getting good pdf from them. So there was that first piece, typesetting. Then, conversion, and generally just doing odd jobs, and finally there was the whole print-on-demand processing, which was mainly going on in Pune, with DPS, which became ValueChain.

The decision to capture XML coding (Books) was made after we were already typesetting offshore?

Yes. Again, that was a decision that was way ahead of its time, and probably wasted a lot of money, I suspect.

Maybe it has yet to pay off? As I see it the devices on which our XML is read now aren't capable of doing the XML justice.

The reason it all went that way is because there was a fantastic level of expertise in the Printing Division that came over to me through redundancies when the typesetting packed up, and there were some really clever people who were committed to XML. In particular, there was Chris Hamilton-Emery, who was an XML junkie. And there were a lot of people within our Indian suppliers who wanted to get on with that, Techbooks particularly. So it was driven from within and without at the same time. Then Andy Williams, whom I hired in, was very committed to that idea as well. But there was a real cost in every single page being done that way.

Well that's another question I wanted to ask you, but which you may not be able to answer: The reduction in the cost of typesetting when moving offshore. Presumably there was an instant and considerable reduction in typesetting page prices?

Oh yes. I've always argued that we didn't necessarily go offshore because it was cheaper. That was a reasonable part of it, but they were just so much better at it and quicker and less arrogant than UK suppliers. And it was an escape, from my perspective, from the Printing Division. You could pay £20 or £30 a page for typesetting – and for really high-spec, technical typesetting, with apparatus and maths, etc., you'd pay £25 a page. There are plenty of people now doing straight-text publishing, getting perfect typesetting from a Word file for $1 a page. When I left the Press it was still vastly more than I felt it should be and vastly more, possibly because of the XML, than other people were paying. That combination of digital printing, xerographic short-run printing, and the reduction in typesetting, and the fact that authors deliver content on disk, means that books are all longer. That's interesting. We did a bit of analysis on that once, to try and see if you could detect any trend, and the most obvious trend in the transition from the typewriter was a very self-evident thing. When you're using a typewriter there's a penalty for insertion, in that, at a certain point of insertion, you'll have to retype the whole page. You look at your page and decide that you want to put things in. Well, you can insert a certain amount by hand – the only way you can do it – but then you reach the point where you want to put in a lot and therefore you retype the whole page and it becomes a page and a half and you repaginate manually. And that was such a slog that people just didn't do it. Now, there is absolutely no penalty for constant insertions of new material, so all the books are 15% longer than they used to be. That's genuinely true. The average book just went up and up in length.

Fascinating.

Yes. What I was saying is that if you didn't have digital printing, delivery of Word files or the offshore element, most academic publishing would not be viable because of the collapse in the market – and the artificiality of the market – sustained somewhat by the Press. There's a book, a long, learned piece which Richard (Fisher) should write because he's so good at all this stuff, about the 1970s and '80s, and that first wave of massified higher education. When I was a student in the late '60s it was maybe two per cent of the population going to university. And when I started work in the 1970s, that first cluster of new universities in the UK was massively increasing participation. You had Keele, Lancaster, and

Essex, Southampton, and Stirling, all these absolutely greenfield universities being built from muddy fields. This generated a huge explosion in academia, academic staff, PhDs, and research, which led to the proliferation of monographs, which hadn't really existed before: people doing specialised stuff, which we then published and the university libraries bought mainly to help peoples' careers. I think Richard would argue that people will look back and see that the novel, something invented in the 17th century, is still going strong, while the serial novel was invented in X and died out in Y. And that the academic monograph was something very weird that started to happen in 1965 and was really over by around 1995. The whole idea of doing these things and printing them on paper is so bizarre.

The monograph print runs are coming down all the time. What was the typical monograph print run, say, when you joined the Press?

I think it would have varied very much in terms of subject. The Science ones to the extent that they were happening were very small, but the better subjects, things like Classics, bits of History, bits of English Literature still weren't enormous, but something like 1200 or 1500, runs like that.

That's enormous compared to the numbers being printed now.

Yes. When I was doing monographs in the early '70s, I was working for a London academic publisher, you could certainly print 2,000 and try and sell 750 or 1,000 as physical books to an American publisher, who would pump them straight into libraries. It was completely ridiculous. The unforgiving thing about digital libraries is you can see if people actually read the books or not. There will be out there, hundreds and thousands of Cambridge monographs on library shelves that nobody has ever touched, just that some librarian had thought they were worth buying.

Possibly very true! I've wondered whether the Academic Books output increased as a result of digital technology. I don't think that it did, but can you recall the numbers being produced?

I don't think it made much difference and why would it?

The money saved, perhaps, in the production process, could result in reinvestment in the list?

I think the money saved just made things work. It's extraordinary that all these lucky things came together to save something which, fundamentally, made no sense, and still makes no sense. It doesn't make sense at all for the output of academic endeavour to be presented like that, when it ought to be a multiple, cross-linked, interactive multimedia, online experience. There's so many things we thought about doing, that still haven't happened. And one of those things is interactive cross-referencing. One of the most basic things, a thought right from the beginning, was – and think about how basic this is – you would insist that authors of academic books, at the point of accessing the bibliographic details of this other book, would never ever do so without including the SBN. It doesn't matter where it goes in the text. Ideally it's in the bibliography, but it doesn't matter. That could then be hidden in the XML as a link and then you have this perfect, unique identifier: the ISBN, which can be sent off to any engine you like. Even if all you're ever actually going to do is an online version, you get some highlighted information, even if it takes you to Amazon, and you've got the full bibliographic information, availability, price, etc. Even better, you're taken to Google Books and the actual text. It's such an easy thing to do, yet that was a failure of Editorial nerve. Exactly the same as how we so struggled to force authors to write synopses of chapters, blurbs for chapters.

You said that this was a frustration right from the beginning. When were you thinking of this cross-referencing functionality?

Right from the very beginning, when we were developing CAMML, and thinking of what functionality we wanted.

I'm very conscious of the time passing and don't want to hold you. Could I perhaps ask you a question or two from the list I sent you earlier?

Of course.

Can you recount your level of understanding at the time of what the DPR in its infancy could mean for academic publishing? It seems to be that you had a high understanding of the potential. Was that you alone?

An awful lot of it was, I'm afraid. I was in a very fortunate position with what Richard Fisher has described as 'Team Holdsworth'. I had total authority. I had reasonable access to budgets. Equally, and life comes full circle to some extent, what I did – and you talked about unifying Press systems – was take the view that Cambridge uniquely could provide, whether it's ELT, Academic or Journals, a world with no boundaries. There is no sense, as there is in trade publishing, of a divide between the US and the UK educational markets. Basically, in the perfect world you have a maths editor and you have just one of them. You don't have a maths editor here and one in New York. You have a maths editor who is just as likely to crop up in a conference in Manila, São Paulo, Chicago, or Vienna, That's what the academics are doing: it's a world community of academics. The academic who's a professor in New York one minute can be in Oxford the next. That's how you need to do it and that would mean that the books should never look any different. You should never be able to tell, be it by price or design, where the book was published. You need to make sure that your editors all behave exactly the same way. They do their contracts and Syndicate papers in the same way and enter information in to databases, ensuring that marketing blurbs are the same. And that meant setting up a system for Cambridge where there was no transfer pricing – Branches weren't selling books to each other.

There was just a body of stock, which was either in one place or another, freely moving between them. It was entirely, in modern parlance, 'group-based' businesses despite starting out from a system whereby all the financial systems in place in New York, Melbourne and Cambridge had been different. Distribution systems were different and the software used was different. Getting all that uniformly in to Vista, which was an amazingly revolutionary thing, again in the late 1970s and early '80s... It was the first time that any such system existed in publishing. It could integrate warehousing with royalties, with Production and Finance and Sales. It was an extraordinary thing that all of this could be tied together in one programme whereas before there were different, cludgy packages at the very beginning of computerisation.

The sales ledger could be the same as the system used for booking books into the warehouse, completely integrated. To get Vista into Cambridge, New York and then Melbourne, and then to try and think about integrating all the other editorial and marketing Filemaker systems was going entirely in the opposite direction to Oxford where, basically – and this is probably the secret, in some ways, to their success – every single part of the Press was allowed to flourish and do their own thing, running their own businesses. They all hated each other and you had a situation where, genuinely, the editor for physics in New York would be fighting the one in Oxford for the same book. They'd almost be turning up at conferences having their own booths. So that, basically, was my vision. I was allowed to get on with all of that. From being very topsy turvy and organic to being very regimented and to be able to say something like 'This is how a copyright page is to look', and that would be absolutely globally defined. That would be the copyright page that everybody will use and would list the cities in one order, for instance. Anybody can pick up an OUP New York book and tell it from an OUP Oxford book, just by looking at it. You shouldn't be able to do that with Cambridge.

My wife was an editor at the Press, in Anthropology. She worked in Cambridge, then she worked in New York for seven years, and then came back. There was no argument about who'd pay for the transfer, 'whose cost/balance sheet is she on?', or 'whose are the editor's books when they move backwards and forwards?' These were the fights we used to have in the very latter days. It was all very silly. But the real success of Oxford is that they were prepared to invest in publishing. I don't think there was a question that we were investing in other things, we just weren't investing in publishing.

I don't think, considering the size of OUP, that they've been much phased by the problem they're now facing with their content and its lack of organisation, because that can be fixed retrospectively.

Yes. I don't think that the things are connected in any way. You can over-specify things and I think, probably, we did – everybody used to think that certain things we did were absolutely amazing. A lot of it was a bit too clever by half.

Michael, we've been talking for over an hour. Thank you. I could happily listen to you talk about this for a very long time.

If you have any specific questions I'll try and remember for you. Some of this stuff ought to be properly documented and of course it isn't at all. I've no idea when so many things actually happened. Most of its only in the last fifteen years, but it's so difficult to remember exactly what came before what!

Are you not inclined to write the history yourself?

Not really! Michael Black has written this book, 'How to be a

Publisher', and that's such an extraordinary exercise in recall more than anything else. Did he write it all down? Did he keep diaries?

His History, his concise history of the Press, ends in 1984, at the beginning of all this. It's remarkable.

Appendix B

Transcript of interview with Pauline Ireland
Friday, 30th March 2012
Telephone conversation 21.00 (GMT)

_____

*Perhaps you could start by describing the production processes
in place at the Press prior to desktop publishing. How was a
typical AcPro book produced exactly?*

I joined the Press in '85 and I was in Journals until '89. Pretty much
exclusively, Journals used UPH for typesetting and if we used
outside typesetters or editorial offices, that was because it was a
proprietor journal and it was their choice to use someone else or
to create camera-ready copy, as it was in those days, themselves.
Journals was strictly UPH. I've been talking to an ex-colleague,
who came up through Printing and, after Rod Mulvey retired, he
ran TAG for a while. That's Chris Mckeown. His father used to
run Typesetting, and Chris did an apprenticeship at the Press so he
has a wealth of knowledge about all this. I wanted to check some
of my thoughts and dates with him and he's been very, very good.
In fact, I think he quite enjoyed it. A 'rave from the grave', sort of.
Did you come across Rod Mulvey?

Only by name. I'm not even sure of his dates, exactly.

TAG morphed into Content Services, basically, and then Content
Services was run by Andy Williams. That's one of the great
tragedies of the Press, that we lost Andy. I became the Design
and Production manager for STM in '89, most of Books, and
I'm talking just of Academic because Learning has always been
different. I think Learning possibly came to desktop publishing
before anyone else. When I started in STM (Books), they weren't
using the Printing House, UPH, at all for typesetting because

their prices were very expensive. It was high-end typesetting. When I was in Journals, I used to watch the proof-readers and those guys were absolutely astonishing. They could pick up an incorrect formula, knowing nothing about the subject matter, but because they had been looking at this stuff for years, they knew when it was wrong and they would call it out. It was absolutely astonishing, but it was a way of working that had to go because it was way too expensive.

In Books [STM], they used a multitude of outside typesetters, most of them using proprietary systems, which of course meant that you could never retrieve the files because the systems ceased to be supported by the people who had sold them as they went out of business... I cut the number of typesetters right back. I was using people like Servis, who are still around, Wyvern, Roland – those people moved in to desktop publishing out of necessity because it became sexy. It was the thing to do. It also gave people a lot of flexibility. Let me give you an example. In 1989, the Press published the first of the IPCC Climate Change Reports. The content was created by the Met office, and we did the whole thing from a standing start in six weeks, which was, in those days, unheard of. We took Pagemaker files from the Met Office when nobody had seen Pagemaker and I needed to top and tail them: I needed to tidy these pages up before we could print the camera-ready copy out. There used to be what was called the Drawing Office, and they used to create artwork and strip artwork in to camera copy. They mainly worked on Journals, but they did a little bit of Book work. I had to sit over there for hours. There were widows and orphans. They were trying to make my down-and-dirty pages from the Met Office in to a Rolls Royce! You can tell this is seared on my memory. People became intrigued, I think, by desktop publishing because it gave them flexibility. What Chris says is "I believe we set TAG up in 1989 and before that the group came under the guise of Netherhall Software. The scope of TAG was to look at using manuscripts that had been keyed using any type of computer. Back then work was supplied on tape, disk (5¼", 8") and the variety was endless. We used an Intermedia disk reader that had some facility to read different sizes/formats and would allow the user to define translation tables that enabled the content to be converted into a different system. This system was used for a number of years until there was a gradual move to Word and Wordstar (this soon disappeared as Word became dominant). As Word became more dominant so too did TeX".

Now, this was my involvement with TAG: I didn't use them for desktop publishing. I used them, when in STM and later when I moved to the States, for topping and tailing TeX and LaTeX files because, of course, in STM, most of the mathematical and physical science books were coming in typeset by the authors, but we needed frontmatter and we sometimes needed indexes [sic], because the author didn't know how to code. So we would do a lot of work with TAG. When I moved to the States, I moved that work from TAG, because they were too slow, unfortunately – and too expensive – to what was then Techbooks, later Aptara. And that was how the Press started working with Aptara. I'm afraid it's all my fault! [laughs] We started working with Aptara in 1994/'95. Prior to this, TAG was doing the TeX topping and tailing. [Referring to Chris Mckeown's notes] "TAG soon became recognised as a leading (supplier) in TeX/LaTeX and a lot of physics and maths books went through this pagination system. Alongside TeX, TAG also introduced Quark and then InDesign to the production process within Cambridge Printing Division". Then he gives you a list of the customers: "The Printing Division worked with some of the leading academic publishers including Wiley, Blackwell, Springer, Elsevier, Hodder & Stoughton, Addison Wesley, Chambers, Chapman & Hall, Routledge, and Taylor & Francis, plus work from the Publishing Division. Alongside this they worked with some very prestigious societies such as The Royal Society, London Mathematical Society, The Biochemical

Society, The Society for General Microbilogy, plus others". Your other question was 'What was the phototypesetting system in place at CUP prior to dtp and the first Macs?', well, "the first Computer Aided Composition system (as we called it back then) was introduced to the Printing House in collaboration with the University Computer department and text was run out to long galleys and then cut into pages in the Paper Makeup department". Back in the day, the Printing House was completely different. There were these huge rooms: the Drawing Office, the Page Makeup department, the Proof-reading department, then of course there were the typesetters. It was enormous. It was giant. And, of course, there were the printing and binding works. It was a very different world... Anyway, "these galleys were run out through Monotype Lasercomps and the Printing House was one of the first to get a Lasercomp in the UK. To get to the next level, and under pressure from one or two customers, the Printing House used the Interset pagination system, which was developed by a company in Somerset. This system enabled Cambridge Printing to offer automatic pagination".

That was a huge deal: automatic pagination. "This system was also introduced to the Pitt Building as well" – Chris used to run that little printing works down in the Pitt Building – "After a while (and he hasn't got a date but I could probably dig it up for you) SGML was introduced and Cambridge Printing developed its own in-house system that ultimately ended up being called CATS. This was a fully automatic pagination system that required tagging of the content to identify the different elements and was a very successful pagination engine for its time, even by today's standards. When this system was introduced there was also a requirement to output SGML as well". He is confirming my impression that desktop publishing was brought in largely due to customer demand and because the automated systems were not flexible enough to produce non-uniform page layout. This was particularly true for Learning. And, of course, once they got desktop publishing, designers could go crazy – which they did! He's got the staffing levels, he says: "When TAG first started there was a team of about seven or eight and grew to about 25 before the group then became part of the main typesetting team in the Printing House" (but I think it must have shrunk again, I can't remember), "It was a very different group (largely) compared to the traditional tradesmen that had been doing the work for years and with it came the usual integration issues of new versus old". Then he says: "Typesetting started drifting away from the Printing House in the early 90's – some of this loss was replaced by new DTP work. In 1999 I made the first trip to India to visit potential partners, but it was quite obvious that the "potential partners" would soon be doing all the work due to their low cost structure and large skills base. Gradually, from 2000–2003, more and more work went offshore to India and operators in Cambridge Printing were really only doing a validation and tidying up role. To me this is when composition really stopped at CUP. There continued to some work on the Macs, but as a serious typesetting operation it was finished". One of the questions you asked was about tagging and I'm getting the impression that you think that the Press wasted an awful lot of time playing around with desktop publishing instead of diving in to tagging at an earlier stage.

Yes, I had thought that the Press had got to grips with SGML and then had become distracted, due to outside pressure, perhaps, by desktop publishing.

No. I went to an SGML conference in Boston in 1996 so there were those of us who were very keen to be tagging our content because it was already happening in Journals. By this time we were publishing a Journal called *Protein Science*, which we didn't own but it was the first online journal that we ever published, and it was run out of New York. We set up a unit in New York called the Electronic Publishing Development Unit and I had someone working in there who had come straight from Brown University, where she had been immersed in SGML. She could write DTDs and so on. We had experience in New York of SGML and publishing online, and of course Cambridge Journals Online went live in the mid 90's. This stuff was going on, but it wasn't going on in Books. I think it was 1996 when Michael Holdsworth set up a group of people called the Computer Integrated Publishing Initiative, latterly known as C(h)IPPI: Rufus Neal, Kevin Taylor, me, and Laura Dorfman (she was a major player) and a bunch of other people. Laura and I were the US representatives. We started doing some experimentation, but of course pdf came in and everything got blown out of the water. "We don't need to do anything – pdf is the answer to all our questions". By this time, I'm suicidal, wanting to stick my head in a gas oven.

That's true. Only in the last couple of years, the typescripts that went out to authors were in XML and the authors were required to code. I can see how that might have been difficult.

Yes. For the most part, they were getting hard copy, obviously, but they had to use this very complicated system for creating their indexes. If they did it properly, it worked beautifully, but, you know, we had letters to Stephen Bourne – "What are you trying to do to me??!". Cathy Felgar is a really good source for you, for information on how all that got sorted out.

It really wasn't a case of 'nobody in Books cared' about tagged content. We did care. We just had no way of getting there. Once Michael (Holdsworth) got involved, essentially, he became *el facto*, *el supremo* of Production, which he didn't really want to be, so it sort of got pushed over to me and to Andy. Things prior to that were disparate: everybody did their own thing. That had to stop because we knew we could save a lot of money, and we knew we'd put efficient workflows in place. That was really quite an exciting time, getting things up and running and sorted out. We were a good team: Andy and me, Cathy Felgar, and people in the UK who were deeply involved. And there was a nice continuity because Andy ran Content Services as well, so that made a big difference. It made things smoother. Ultimately, I don't know what the role of Content Services will be because it's changed dramatically from when it started.

True. I think it's largely focused on validating content now. I imagine then, that with desktop publishing, the focus went to print. The importance of coding was understood, it just hadn't been implemented by that point.

Yes, that's right. The significance and importance of coding had been understood by... pockets of knowledge, but there wasn't any continuity. TAG were involved, with the systems that they put in – they did get in to the SGML world and, as I said before, Journals were there before anyone else. We've had Cambridge Journals Online live since 1996, but it was, what, two years ago before we got Cambridge Books Online. I was involved with CJO from the New York end, which was great, and then I was involved with CBO and that, I have to say, was probably – apart from running the project of moving our offices from West 20th down to Tribeca – the most fun I've ever had at the Press: Cambridge Books Online. It was absolutely terrific. An amazing experience, and we did it so quickly. A great team. Michael (Holdsworth) drove innovation because he was, and probably still is, a visionary. He could see the future. It was wonderful to work with him because he would always listen to new ideas and he'd help us try to get innovation started. Working with Michael and Andy was terrific, it really was. It was cutting edge and we had a good time. But getting to that point was difficult.

Do you think that the Press, at the time desktop publishing took hold, was following or leading the industry in the UK?
Ooh. Well, which bit? Publishing or Printing?

Well, Printing?

73

Printing were always innovating with new technology. There were always new machines and systems being put in. The problem was that there wasn't an overall strategy to bring the bits together. Even their internal systems, as I said earlier, couldn't talk to one another. The Press as an organisation must have thrown away... I can't bear to think about how much they threw away, putting in a back-office system on one side of the road that didn't talk to the back-office system on the other side. They were run as two separate businesses, but the savings that could have been made were tremendous. There was a cutting edge. I don't know whether their desktop publishing was necessarily cutting edge. Chris might have a different take on it.

Pauline, thank you. We've been talking, or rather, you've been talking for more than 40 minutes and I've been listening, avidly. I can't thank you enough. I'm extremely appreciative.

Transcript of interview with Chris Mckeown
Wednesday, 4th April 2012
Edinburgh Building, Room 2, 12.00pm

On the introduction of Computer Aided Composition...

When we first started doing the computerised composition, Computer Aided Composition, I was just finishing my apprenticeship. I did an apprenticeship in hot metal and CAC was introduced in 1980. We were still doing hot metal then and gradually phased in the CAC. It was an interesting time. Very interesting. You had computers that took up the size of this wall here, filling a room to do what this [points at iPad] can do. The big tapes and ICL disk drives: huge machinery.

So it was a gradual introduction?

It was. I suppose from 1980 up to 1990. I'd say it was laboured. Very hard to see any improvements. Then, all of a sudden, when the big manufacturers like Monotype and Linotype got involved, there were new systems springing up. It moved at quite a pace. I remember, back in 1990, going to a meeting to do with SGML. That was the first meeting to do with SGML that I went to. There was a load of typesetters and a few SGML experts – it was actually chaired by the CUP head designer at the time, a chap called John Trevitt. I remember the typesetters all standing up, you know, from all over the UK, saying "this will never work! No-one's going to pay for SGML. It's so labour intensive, etc. etc." It was pooh-poohed right from the outset by the typesetters.

What was in place before that time?

Well, each typesetter had their own system: there was Miles – Miles are still going, obviously they're fully XML now – there was Interset, Linotype, Monotype, Petta, and all that was required was output to film or bromide, through a Linotype or Monotype device. Phototypesetting. CUP had, I think, the first Monotype Lasercomp in the UK. We eventually ended up with three of them. That did seem to happen quite quickly.

It was a huge change.

It *was* a huge change. And the very first system that we had was actually written by the Computer Lab down in the University. There was a chap called Neil Wiseman and that's when the Printing House started employing its own computer 'expert', as they were known then. A programmer. A head programmer to help develop the system. It was typical CUP at the time. It was playing with it – it had money, resources… When you look back at it now, it's hard to believe that it was cutting-edge technology! The screens were really big, the green cathode type, I remember the guys having to work with a big tracker ball, as the mouse, to move the cursor round the screen.

And this was used for rekeying manuscripts, coding them essentially?

Yes. Everything was tagged, you know, angle-bracket coding. Primitive SGML/XML-type coding: begin tag/end tag. And that just got developed and enhanced all the way through the typesetting developments, from day one.

And we're still going, really.

And here we are with XML that has just gone on from each of those tagged processes. Typesetters had their own systems. CUP always wanted to have their own unique system, which you could say was a good point, or you could say a downfall.

This was before Word?

This was when Word came on board. Basically, what happened… let's go back and put this in order… From our first system, the one developed by the University Computing Lab – to be honest, I don't remember much of that because I wasn't involved at that stage, having just finished my apprenticeship. They were big mainframes, taking up a huge amount of space, but at the time it was cutting-edge technology. It was a coded system and back then, at the start, we weren't making up pages – we were running out galleys. From the galleys you would run out bromide galleys through the phototypesetters and then it would go into Paper Makeup, where everything would be cut and pasted. The pages got waxed, cut and put on to a backing sheet, and then photographed by the Opticopy. A monster of a device. Then the film would be plated from there. Going back to our first typesetting system, this was way before the Opticopy. A good ten years or so before, could have been fifteen years before. Once we got that first system up and running, then it was just a series of developments. Either new hardware, or software to upgrade each year, or every other year, but it was always our own system and that's when the Printing House started employing computer programmers.

I think it's fair to say that, back in those times, these were pretty strange guys. It was a new field and they were usually very, very bright people. So, the system got developed. There was a chap called John Naylor, he was in charge at the last phase of it and John did a good job to get us up to SGML – for the system to produce SGML in as automated a way as could be done at that time. This is going back to the 2000 mark, plus or minus. TAG was set up because we (i.e. the Publishing Division) had started receiving stuff on disk. Initially, people used to get the disk and throw it away and just copy-edit the manuscript as normal, send it over and it got rekeyed. Then we started asking the question "This has come from a computer. Can we have the computer disk". That's when we got the Intermedia disk reader. That was a wonderful device. It could read anything: the Amstrad disks, which were 3 inch, not 3½ inch, they were odd sizes, then the 5¼, then the 8-inch disks, and then the 3½-inch, hard-cased things, and then… zip something, drives? All sorts of drives came in, but the Intermedia disk reader was a very versatile device. It would enable you to read WordStar, Word – all the different versions – and there were multiple other word-editing tools available as well. It would show you the codes to put bold on or bold off, etc., and you could then write a script, a very simple translation table, so 'look for this and convert it to this'.

So you were converting to the coding that you wanted. We actually used that to convert material to go in to Quark, or into Word and then into Quark. We primarily used it for books and journals going in to our own typesetting system. We could write rules like 'if you find this and it falls within this area, then it becomes this, but if it falls outside this area, it becomes this code'. At the time, they were complex rules to govern what you tagged. That was a very good system. We used that in conjunction with the Interset system, which was a complete system.

What exactly was it, the Interset pagination system?

It was a complete typesetting system, including complete pagination. So you would generate a PostScript file that you would send to a Lasercomp, or to a filmsetter, and run out completed pages. It was automated with manual intervention. So you could say "actually, I don't like that illustration there". Very much like Quark and InDesign: "I want it there". You set up a whole set of rules, defining the spacing above and below headings, above and below illustrations; it was a very good system. And we trialled it because we were under pressure at the time from one customer, a Society, actually, the *Fluid Mechanics* journal, which pushed us down that route. They were saying "why aren't you doing things automatically?", and so we had to appease them because, back then, you would be getting something in the region of £40/£50 a page. I wish we were getting that now! £3/£4 a page now gets you everything. I know that we were charging £100 a page when we were doing hot metal. That was the standard price. So, the Intermedia was a great tool for encouraging publishers to send in work to typesetters on disk. Typesetters would use the disks to bring it in to their systems, and everybody had their own route for doing that. I would say the Interset system came in just before or around DTP, and it was very much aimed at the Academic market: books and journals, not the magazines/occasional ELT-type product, which is really where, as I saw it, the DTP side of things was. When the first Macs were introduced in the Printing House, we used them for drawing artwork.

That was where their real use came in over there. Over here, in Publishing, I think the designers thought they had died and gone to heaven! You then stated getting – yes, I will say – stupid requests from designers like "I want 9¾ point on 11.25 leading". At that time, bearing in mind the designers were designing on a Mac but the product's being output on a more traditional system, not on a Mac, that did result in some pretty heated 'discussions': Production versus the designer. I was quite hot on typography. I looked after all the fonts over there, and the requests coming through from designers were really pretty ludicrous. There was no benefit at all in saying "I want 9¾ point on 11.3 leading", you know. And then of course they started asking for feathering and leading and stuff like that, which was a big 'no no' in traditional typesetting. That's when the two clashed.

How was that clash rectified?

[Laughs] I do remember my father, who was the director of composition, calling over one particular designer who came up with a rather odd request and telling her in no uncertain terms what a load of crap she'd asked for. That was one way of resolving it! The other was trying to educate the designers that what they're asking for isn't realistic. And then they would come up with quite quirky designs for books, designs that the system couldn't deliver. So, it was "okay, you've got a WYSIWYG tool that can do all these whizzy things but it's not automated, you can't use it for mass production and these are tools that all the typesetters in the UK are using". Some were using Macs, but really for very design-orientated work, not your everyday Academic & Professional book. So that took a lot of headbanging to work it all out. Quite often a spec would come over and would go back saying "Can't do this, this, and this. This is what we can offer...". And that's how it worked for the early stages of DTP. We then introduced the DTP side of things in TAG to offer another service to the non-traditional Academic work we were doing. We started doing more illustrated work than we'd done before. This was done in Quark.

I take it that was predominantly for external customers, and not just Publishing?

We had a lot of external customers. I've listed some of them for you. Cambridge Printing at that time was very independent, with a big reputation for quality and service. Having those external customers at that time was important because it gave balance. There was very much an 'us and them' perspective between Printing and Publishing.

It makes sense, I suppose, for a high-end independent printer and typesetter to have such high-end customers.

Yes, it ran as a separate entity. Obviously it was influenced by Publishing and over the years they grew closer together. And a lot of investment was guided by Publishing, like machine sizes: "What book formats do you want? Okay, we'll buy this press and that will do 60% of your work". When TAG was set up we probably had two or three DTP operators and two or three LaTeX or TeX operators, and we ended up with eight or nine DTP operators, and the same number on TeX.

Was TeX being done here prior to TAG?

Hmm. Just. It was being investigated, I would say. The Netherhall Software bit – which was a bit of an odd set up, we're not really sure quite what they did – they were set up originally at the Netherhall School, I believe, and then they were bought by Cambridge, set up in Printing, and didn't really do a great deal. Didn't really succeed as Netherhall Software. They had a guy who was playing around with TeX and then it was decided that TAG would be formed, coinciding with material coming in on disk. There were a couple of programmers, a couple of operators, myself, as a supervisor, and Rob Mulvey who headed the group. The software guys did some programming, but as it became a Production unit, they weren't playing a very big role so they disappeared and it became a development group aligned with Production, [focused] on getting material in.

That's when it grew through a few changes in staff, the introduction of women (!): Brenda, Jane, and Sandra. There had been some women keyboard operators. When we first went over to CAC, we had computers just for keyboarding and we introduced some women there, which was quite a big step. It wasn't normal to have women in printing. It took some of the guys a lot of getting used to. I know for a fact there were disciplinary meetings along the way! It was tough going! We also had a couple of ladies involved with the LaTeX. Then TAG got integrated in to mainstream Composition because it was growing and growing and the people in mainstream Composition needed to know about it and how to handle it, so that material that come in on disk could be handled by 'the team' as opposed to TAG.

Was 'mainstream Composition' the unique typesetting system?

Yes. By then it was CATS. Cambridge Advanced Typesetting System.

Was CATS a direct move from CAC?

It changed in to it. There was no physical change, apart from TAG moving to the mainstream Composition. We still had LaTeX and DTP sections as well as our own system. Basically, we operated three systems.

Were these all using Interset?

No. The Interset system didn't last that long. It actually spurred the programmer on to develop our system to do pagination.

Which was CATS.

Yes, but there was another version of our system before CATS. They never had names, apart from CATS. Interset was brought in to appease a customer; the programmer learnt a lot from it and developed our own system. That system then got upgraded, probably two or three times over the course of ten years, and ultimately became CATS.

This is automatic pagination. What about imposition?

It wasn't doing imposition. It would send pages to Noel's crew in electronic format. And they would make it up for the Computer to Plate. Initially we would send bromide or film pages to the Opticopy then the Opticopy would shoot it in 8s or 6s, or whatever the format was. The film was taped together, then plated. After the Opticopy came Computer to Plate. The [typesetting] system would squirt out electronic files, PostScript files, to the [CTP] system and it would pick up the coding.

Going back to SGML, I'm still unclear as to 'when'. Is it possible to pin-point when SGML was being produced by the systems?

It was about 1995ish. Must have been. Maybe even a bit earlier. I remember [laughs] that everyone was asking for SGML but nobody was doing anything with it. They'd archive it. This particular customer, for whom we were producing SGML – and we thought it was fine – about two years down the line, they went to use the SGML and check it all and it wasn't quite as it should have been. We had to retrospectively go back and put it all right. Everybody was jumping on the SGML bandwagon but they didn't know why they wanted it, and they had nothing to do with it. It was years before any of them could do anything with it. Obviously it's a precursor to XML, but nobody really had an SGML front-end system compared to the XML front-end systems that we have now. SGML was produced as a by-product. Everything was post-processed. Publishing was never the first to ask for a particular product. In a lot of cases, we were driven by external customers.

When did Word take over from WordStar?

God. Certainly way before the end of TAG. TAG moved into CAC to become one room. The Interset pagination system was a system that we just brought in. It was actually a bit of a leper in that it was unique and we only ran one or two journals through it. Well, four journals, but all for the same customer, the Royal Society – very prestigious journals to typeset. I was basically running that, off in a room on my own.

Would this have been the first WYSIWYG system?

Certainly one of the first. I'm trying to think whether it came in alongside the Macs. It may have come just before actually. Let's say 'around the same time'. Interset didn't change – it influenced the workflow in as much as it was a system that our technical people used to see how it worked in order to develop the CUP 'home-grown' system.

Do you remember if it had a WYSIWYG viewer? And could you use this live, in real time?

Yes, it did. You had a split screen: WYSIWYG/coding. SGML was not the basis for CATS. We already had our own unique coding system and basically the SGML coding was mapped to the back of it. We had our own coding, such as: an A Heading in our system was <SSHA>, a main category, then <SSHB>, and it was very much like the early days of DTDs because we would have what we called a Job Description – it was quite a good set up. For example [writing] we'll call this JD Book 1: each Job Description was named, whether the journal acronym of the book title. So, <SSHA> would have a description in JD Book 1, including font, size, leading, all the information you needed, text, extracts, and the same for <SSHB>. So every job was coded in exactly the same way. If you put in FLJD (Fluid Mechanics Job Description), it would take the FM journal Job Description and impose it on those codes and it would come out looking like a journal. A very powerful system.

That's generic coding, of course.

Yes, but these codes were not SGML. These were typesetting codes, which we developed. Then, to get to SGML, you had to post-process. These codes were mapped to their relevant SGML codes.

So CATS put the content being produced by the Printing House in to really good shape for SGML?

Yes. We did have to change some of the things we did here to enable the post-processing. To be totally honest with you, Tom, how successful we were at that, I'm not sure…! Was it 80%, 90%, 95%? I don't know.

It wasn't being QA'd?

It was towards the end when customers started to have a use for it. But not many of them. There's probably some CUP SGML floating around out there that has never been checked! This [indicating CUP generic coding] was developed way before SGML was even thought of. CUP Printing was ahead of its time in that respect. I believe that this was a very good system because you had standard coding throughout all the journals. No matter what journal you picked up, as an operator, you knew that <SSHA> was a main heading. I wrote a C programme – a syntax checker – to check that within <SSHA> you couldn't have any <SSEQ> [equation elements], basically to make sure that you coded it – and at the time the operators were keying on computers and sending it across to the mainframe to be picked up: we were still doing a lot of manual keying, a hell of a lot. I would have been around 26/27 when I wrote that because I remember I was getting loads of overtime, which I needed because I'd just bought a flat!

So that would have been about 1985. Around that time, we had this [CUP generic coding] in place. The syntax checker enabled the operators to detect mistakes they had made in their coding. But I was despised by the operators because they thought I was checking on their work, and it would affect their bonus because they'd have to go back and put that work right.

What an introduction to the Press! But the very fact that a syntax checker was necessary means that it would have been quite an infant system at that point. If you're saying this was 1985ish, then it's early eighties really, isn't it?

Oh yes. That was a great project to work on. I got a load of over-time out of it and I needed it! You can relate everything back to, you know…

Milestone events!

As I say, it's hard to remember exactly where the Interset system fitted in in relation to the introduction of DTP typesetting. Was it just before, just after, during? I'm pretty sure it was just before, or just at the very outset. The Interset was a Frome-based company down in Somerset. They were selling the system but I actually went down there and stayed down there for several weeks, to help them develop it.

For Cambridge?

And for them to sell on. My area of expertise was traditional type-setting and pagination, so I could pick holes in the system from a pagination point of view. For instance, the system could go back one or two pages when actually it needed to go back to the start of the article, and then repaginate, depending on the requirement. But the thing then was RAM. Memory was too expensive and not available. So that restricted systems in doing that. It wasn't until memory became more available that you could make programmes that were far better. People knew that you needed a system that could go back, but they didn't have the hardware. I mean, RAM is nothing now but then it was a big issue.

That's an exciting project, the Interset consultancy.

Yeah. It was good fun. I learned a lot. It was very interesting. I then got involved in TeX. I wasn't proficient on the coding of it at all, but I understood the principles of what was involved enough to quote the word to annoy Pauline!

And TeX continues.

Yes. Aptara do a hell of a lot of TeX. Thousands of pages a year.

Isn't 3B2 TeX-based?

Well, our pagination (system) is a TeX engine. We have XML first and then flow it in to a LaTeX engine for pagination. So it basically maps on the fly to LaTeX for pagination only without effecting the source code in XML. We use that for a lot of our work. 3B2 uses a TeX engine for pagination in a similar way. It's still very, very widely used.

Were Aptara one of the first to do XML first?

Yes, I think we were. I think Gurvinder, the CTO at the time, was heavily involved and I think Aptara were probably the first offshore vendor to go down an XML workflow. At the time it was a gamble, but it's obviously paid off. It was the right choice. They always tried to push the technology side, always tried to be at the forefront of any new technology and developments. Sometimes to our downfall, sometimes it works. The company has always tried to be one step ahead. At the time, Gurvinder had a very strong relationship with Michael [Holdsworth], and Michael depended on Gurvinder an awful lot.

At that time, it was just Aptara, wasn't it?

Yes, and that was started by Pauline. I remember her phoning me up when she heard I was going to India, saying "are you going to see Techbooks?", and I said "yes", "well it's my supplier and I don't want you peeing them off!". She gave me a right earful! I said, "Pauline, if they want to work with us, they'll work with us". That's when the Printing House started off-shoring work.

Was it a capacity issue?

No, it was a way to reduce our costs. The Printing House was damned expensive. High overheads, high staffing costs, and at a time when some publishers were going direct to offshore, getting much reduced prices compared to dealing on shore. I went over there with Stephen Bourne, on my first visit. He'd only been with the Press for about six months. We went and looked at around four typesetters. Back in 1999, there wasn't the choice that there is now and Techbooks were one of the prominent ones. I came back and had to write a report to my boss, the managing director of Printing, and basically I said that "if we don't use offshore, we're finished". It was as simple as that, as far as I was concerned. And as plain as that. It was obvious. Just the costs and skill base. That was back in 1999 and here we are, thirteen years later, and a hell of a lot of learning has gone on. It wasn't quite as straightforward as, you know, "let's move it offshore". Offshore had a lot to learn. I refer to it as the honeymoon period. Aptara [née Techbooks] has been going since 1988, so twenty years of experience. To me, the honeymoon period is over and publishers expect/demand a certain level of expertise and knowledge and assume that. That's why I think some vendors are struggling, and I include us, having struggled in the last few years. We have found that publishers have become more demanding because the level of expectation is such that "they've been doing this for X number of years, I expect them to know it". Just as you would internal or onshore suppliers: "you should know it by now". And so the tolerance of the fact that it's 'offshore' has gone. There's no leeway now. That's what I've noticed. You stand up and be counted, and deliver what's expected.

And of course the customer, the publisher, is now closely checking these deliverables.
Yes!

Thanks, Chris, so much. This was absolutely great. I'm much obliged.

Appendix D

Transcript of interview with Noel Robson
Wednesday, 22nd February 2012
University Printing House canteen, 14.55pm

I suppose, if you don't mind, we should start from when you started. What was the set-up when you started in 1992?

It was all film. We had the Opticopy camera, which was an imposing camera, running camera-ready copy. You'd mount the camera-ready copy on a strip, put it on a copy board, expose it, shoot her to film, and then the back board would move behind the camera. And then you'd put your next copy up and hit 'fire', then put the next one up, etc., until you'd get 8, 16, or 32 pages on one sheet of film. You had one guy basically pressing the button, one guy in the dark room, one guy out the back of the processor, processing film. You had the Little John camera, where we would create the cover artwork. The cover artwork would come through on a board and we'd shoot it on the camera, make a Neg[ative], and then you'd tint lay it a few different colours, using contact film, and mask different bits out so you'd end up with your separations for your film, for your different colours. The Autocon scanner was a little black and white scanner with infrared that scanned directly to film. You'd take your original, read the densities of your dark and light point, put them into the machine, put it on the bed, click 'go', and it would scan it at those densities and put it straight out to film. And then you'd turn that film into bromides, in a contact frame, and all the imposition work was done by about twenty guys on light tables. So, we had about ten on each shift, imposing all the single-page film to imposed sheets, making those in to proofs, on paper, which were developed through ammonia, and, once the proofs were approved, they would go through to the Platemaking department, where we had six plate frames of various sizes...

What's a plate frame?

It's an exposure frame. You lay your plate down, lay your film on top, close the lid, a vacuum comes up so that it's in tight contact with the plate, and then the UV light exposes it. So, if it's a Neg, it obviously goes through the clear bits and hardens the coating – if it's Pos, it works the other way round and you just develop your plate. Everything was done by hand. There wasn't a single computer in the department.

In 1992?

Yes, in 1992, by which time I was doing my apprenticeship – by block release: we'd go for six–eight weeks at a time – and we're learning DTP, typesetting, those sorts of things. Learning the current stuff and then going back to work and back in time.

Probably a good education.

It was. Very good.

So, that's all camera-ready copy. When did that become electronic?

What, the text, or everything?

Everything.

Around 1996. The camera-ready copy was electronic in a way. It was output to copy because there was no way of processing the electronic files, so it was output to copy and shot on a camera. But it started life as, you know – it was still keyed in to a ticker-tape machine or whatever they used to output it to the paper. In 1996, we bought a Taiga system, made in conjunction with a Japanese company, called Screed, and we bought a drum scanner and a film setter. Basically, the Taiga was a work station for processing files, editing files, imposing files, and outputting to film. We would take in PostScripts, we would scan TIFFs from the scanner directly to the Taiga, do all the work on a Mac, and put the job together on the Taiga.

Like what you do in Quark now, Taiga had its own version of that type of software. It was the first WYSIWYG system: whatever you saw on-screen was what you were going to get out on film. We used to use that primarily for colour, so that would be covers, and colour text jobs. So, that was Quark files [at the time]. We would make Postscripts from the Quark files on the Macs and put them on to the Taiga.

So the Macs came with Quark?

Yeah. We were running old Quadra Macs, pre-Power Mac, and some of the early Power Macs using Quark 3.3, I think. So, it was all Quark. There was nothing else back then: Pagemaker and Quark.

You'd simply run Quark files through the Taiga?

You'd put it all together in Quark, like you do now, and put it in to Taiga to verify it, so that would process it in to a file within Taiga – I'm not sure what format it was, but it would be a ripped file, so you were seeing on-screen the finished file. You could view the separations, the trapping, the colour values – everything. You'd make the corrections and output that to film.

There'd be no change from what you were seeing on the Mac screen and on the Taiga screen?

No, it was the Taiga screen. The Taiga screen was basically the god. You checked it on the Taiga screen, to see if it was right, and then you'd commit to film because there was no electronic proofing back then. You made your proofs from your film. Your ozalids or your chromalins, you'd make from your film. So, for instance, a manual chromalin would take about an hour to do, one chromalin proof.

91

How many pages would that be?

That was one side. One sheet. So, we do an imposed sheet now in about ten minutes, and we just let it run in the background. Back then you'd get your bit of board, you'd laminate the board with a photo-sensitive clingfilm-type thing, you'd then put your bit of film on it, put it in a light frame, expose it with light, so the film protects the sensitive areas and the rest gets burned away. You'd then peel the top layer of cling film off and that leaves a sticky residue that hasn't been exposed. You'd put it through an inking station. So, you'd put it through a Cyan inking station to put your Cyan down. Then you'd have to re-laminate it, lay Magenta foil on in perfect fit, by eye, using the linen tester, do the same for yellow then black, and that would take an hour. And you're not doing anything else: you're just spending an hour making a single proof. If you had a ten sig[nature] job; 20 proofs – that's 20 hours' work just to make the proofs.

If it was a cover, you'd tend to have to do it in Pantone, because most covers were Pantone back then, and we certainly printed in Pantone. You'd have powders, which you'd mix up to make the Pantone colour. You'd have a recipe and you'd mix the powders to make your Pantone. So you'd expose it the same way, peel your top sheet off to leave the sticky image and then you'd dust it. Dust it by hand, blow off the residue, that gives you your colour, and then seal it with another laminate. And repeat it for every colour. That was the first electronic file, at that point. In 1998, all the text, the bulk of the text, was still being done on the cameras. It was still being shot on the Opticopy. The Taiga was mainly for covers, scanning and colour work. At that time, it was used a lot for external work. Because a lot of the Cambridge titles were mono.

So, it wasn't useful for text layout?

You could use it for text layout but it wasn't the friendliest thing. We'd still do text impositions on it but they were quite small, maybe just Z's, so eight pages, maybe 16 if you were lucky. And that would come out of the film setter punched, with holes ready to go on the pins to make your plate or proof. And that was the first time we'd seen imposed film electronically. But it was very dual. I reckon 80% of the work was still hand-planned and 20% was done electronically. Because there was a lot of scanning back then: Everything came in as transparencies – there were no electronic, digital cameras. It was all hard-copy scans. We were scanning 6,000, maybe 10,000 images a year. Maybe even more.

Are you processing more or less now?

Less. Probably 3,500–4,000 images a year now. We saw it start dropping off from about 2000. Once digital cameras came out, there was no need to process [such numbers] as people were happy with what they got from the cameras. That was your final file. Between '96 and '98, we bought another scanner. Just more scanning power really. At that point we had the Autocon scanner, the Horizon scanner – I think – can't remember now, it was an Agfa scanner – and the Screed drum scanner. And ten people, I suppose, running in that area, doing the covers, the proofs, and the scanning. And still about twenty others out on the tables doing hand planning.

So, were those new jobs?

No, they were people moving, retraining. There were a few people employed: we brought a scanner operator in, who was an experienced colour scanner, because we had never done it before. The only people who really knew it were myself and the other apprentice, because we'd done it at college. This guy had years of experience so he was brought in to do colour scanning and then we brought four or five new colour planners in. Because we could now run our own colour film, we needed experienced colour planners to impose the single-page colour film, which we were running more and more of. In 1998 we brought some imposition software called Imposition Publisher, made by Farruk, and that would let us handle PostScripts. We'd get the PostScripts straight from the typesetters or the customer and we would impose them electronically on-screen, and that again would run out to impose and make film. We bought another image setter, so we had two large image setters, one primarily Pos, one primarily Neg. The Taiga would generally run to the Pos, and the Imposition Publisher would run to the Neg via a hardware twin RIP.

So that was the first, free-standing RIP we bought. You'd send your PostScript file to the RIP, your RIP would do all the calculations at that point and send the readable file to the image setter. Imposition Publisher relied on drivers to interpret the PostScripts that came in and it would then create a new file that it would send to the RIP, which had to reinterpret everything Imposition Publisher had done.

You're talking about text files coming in from India?

Back then we used to have a DTP department within Publishing that used to do keying and typesetting here. There's only Brenda Youngman now left from that area. We had a drawing office that would deal with the electronic preparation of files. At the Taiga stage, we'd still receive the so-called 'final' Quark file – so the Drawing Office would have prepared it from scratch. We would then have to process it for press.

That was the beauty of Taiga. You could then see exactly how the different elements reacted with each other. So a lot of it was still being done in-house.

Back here, with Imposition Publisher being used, you were receiving Quark files from the typesetters?

No. PostScripts. We had no way of viewing them at all. You didn't make pdfs back then, there was just PostScript and you had to interpret it properly so it was basically flowed in on-screen and imposed on-screen.

Was there much work at this end, generally?

Not on the text too much, no. The main work was if it didn't process, you'd have to find a new driver or split the file up, play around with it, but you didn't go in to it at code level, which was dangerous. It's miles and miles of code to find one problem. It was generally interpretation problems with the files, more than anything, from random weird packages... Covers caused us more problems just because they hadn't been set up right in the first place.

Where were they coming from?

The Drawing Office, Publishing Division. Back then there was a huge, huge, knowledge divide between what they called the Drawing Office, graphic designers and printers. The printers knew what they needed and how to get it and what they wanted, and the graphic designers didn't know how to set up the file so that it would print correctly. So it was that age old thing where they could make it look how they wanted it to look and we had to print it like that but work out what to do with it so that it could print like that. You'd spend hours sometimes putting a file right. It was a learning process.

Around 2002, the Drawing Office merged with Prepress. We took their front-end skills – they trained us in their front-end skills – and we taught them our prepress skills so we were then creating covers from scratch and processing them at the same time. And that was how our current Reprographics department was formed. It was the merging of the Drawing Office and Prepress departments that made the Reprographics department. The problem with the Harlequin RIP we used to have was, the way it used to work was it had two sides. Files coming in and being ripped, and files being pushed out to the imagesetter. It was a constant feed, imaging as it was being fed data. We used to get these very thing hairlines appearing through the Negs, all the way from top to bottom, and we worked out in the end that it couldn't push and pull at the same time. I can't think of the term, but it was either parallel or non-parallel imaging and it used to run parallel so it's imaging while it's receiving a file and that's when we were getting the little glitches that would miss a line of data out, so you'd just get this blank line appear. Like you'd just scratched the film.

So we then changed it to non-parallel imaging, sending files to it, wait for them to finish ripping – once they'd ripped, you could then output them, but it couldn't process any files while it was outputting. That was the problem with the Harlequin RIP, a very early RIP. I think it was one of the first – when it was developed further it was definitely one of the first RIPS to be able to fully understand transparencies.

Obviously, at that point in time, transparencies didn't exist. If you wanted a special effect, you had to do it the old-fashioned way – in Photoshop, or Taiga was very good at putting drop shadows and things like that on. It was good little beast. Then, in 2000, we moved to Impact software, which gave us more control over the processing of files. We didn't need different drivers, it'd take in pretty much anything and deal with it.

Like a stepping stone to pdf?

Yeah, it could handle pdfs whereas Farruk generally all we used to put through was PostScripts. So yeah, Impact would take Post-Scripts, pdf input as well, very early pdfs, and again just imposed them but it allowed us to be more flexible with printers marks and binders marks to make it easier to print from. But it was the same sort of software really.

In 2001 we got our first platesetter, the Lotum, which was made by Heidelberg at the time. Obviously that had a RIP and you'd send the files to the Lotum PC, that would then rip them out directly to plate. So that was the first real entry-level in to CTP.

How big a change was that to you on the ground? Did a lot of volume go through this to begin with?

The biggest change was when we got Imposition Publisher in 1998–99. That was when the Opticopy went. So we got to see an old piece of kit leaving the building. They shut the Opticopy down, the Little John camera went, plus peoples' jobs because they used to run the cameras. And now everything was coming through as PostScripts, there was no need to run it to camera-ready copy. That was the first time we saw a major change in the structure of Prepress.

The Drawing Office hadn't joined us at this point. It might have been around the same time. I think the Opticopy went first and then we started merging with the Drawing Office, mainly because of all the problems we'd started getting with the files. It was clear they didn't know how to present a file to print correctly so it was just easier to merge and share the knowledge really.

But yeah, the Opticopy was the first big change. Then they reshuffled the actual Prepress department, obviously with a view to getting a platesetter in in a couple of years' time, so they moved plate frames around. When the platesetter came in that was running colour plates for the Speedmaster 8 unit, mono plates for our three Speedmaster 2 units, and cover plates. So at that point they were done on a Favrit, plus I think we'd just got our first Speedmaster 74, a five-unit cover press which we eventually had two of. But there was still a lot of manual film plating because up until this point everything had been film.

So we were still running out to imposed film as well as plates. We were still running some single-page film that had to be imposed. There was still a lot of film coming in from external sources. There were jobs that weren't being supplied as PostScript, you'd get a bag of film come in. They'd run them out of their image setter and send you 500 pages of film. Or, if it was colour, they'd send you 2,000 bits of film that you've then got to start putting together to impose it as colour.

Do you receive anything like that now? Can you handle it?

We've still got the skillset – it's having the capacity. Everyone in Prepress now knows how to do film planning. It's what we grew up on. We still process film now. We still do a small amount of film planning and film plating, but not a lot.

We've still got the facility at the moment, but for how long I don't know because we've obviously got the scanner coming in soon, so that's going to start digitising printed copy so you don't need to go to film anymore to have a digital copy of it. That's probably the last nail in the coffin for film.

That and inkjet printing.

Yeah. So that was when we first got in to platesetting, that as a dual line, if I remember rightly. We had Agfa plates and Poly-chrome plates so they'd come out of the platesetter and, depending on what type of plate it was, it would go left or right for a different processor.

The Lotum?

This is the Lotum, yeah. It had two bays, so you'd have two different plates at a time. We'd set them up as Agfa Plate or Polychrome Plate, and it knew what way to send the plates so it would come out the Lotum, down the conveyor belt and to a turning station where, depending on what plate it was, it would turn left or right and through a processor. One had Agfa chemistry and one had Kodak chemistry.

The processors haven't really changed much – they're much

the same. The same as on the back of the imagesetters, you had processors. In the same way, you'd expose the film, going through a processor. It's basically the same with a platesetter. The platesetter exposes the plate and then it goes out through a processor, so it's developed, washed off, and gummed up, and comes out the back, ready to be stored in the machine room and printed at a later date. So, we still had no large-format platemaking so, in 2002, we bought a Trendsetter, which was a large-format plate device, manual feed, so you'd literally feed one plate in, you'd tip the table, the feed table slides in to the device, takes it around the drum, shuts the lid, you hit 'go', it exposes it, spits it out, you take it off and put it through a processor manually. So, very little automation on that. Again, we'd send the files from Impact to the device. And that was pretty much how we stayed until 2008, when we bought the Kodak Magnussen devices. Two of them, which were fully automated – basically as modern as you could get at the time – state-of-the-art plate devices with four cassettes in each, so four different plate sizes in each one, running around 24 plates an hour.

So they could equip every printing machine?

Yes. Basically two platemaking devices were running the entire machine room. We were running about 120,000 square meters of plate a year, 150 at our peak. As well as still plating for film, if it was a reprint from film. We still had that going on as well. The film was obviously stored – in the film store – I think it was estimated at one point that there was over 50,000 titles in the film store. As well as external jobs, there was the colour film store and the cover film store. Basically, three different film stores. If it came up for a reprint from film, you'd do it from film. Even though we had the plate devices, going back to the Locum and Trendsetters, we had two different devices – we had a team of six people imposing files and we still had a team of six people doing film work. That's how much film work there still was. This is something like 2002. Plus we had the Prepress department, the Scanning department, the Camera department. They were all still around. It was quite a slow change then from 2002 onwards, until everything became pretty much electronic.

Was there a huge variation in staff levels during the ten years between the time you started and 2002?

In all honesty, it probably increased because we took on film planners – we had some film planners come in from London, who were experienced colour-film planners – just because everything used to be pretty basic stuff when I started here. Once we started producing our own colour film, obviously we then were happier to print more colour jobs because we could process them and produce them ourselves – because we used to have to get the film in from somewhere else – so, if we had a colour job, the film was supplied to us as four bits of film for every page and then we'd impose it. Obviously, as the technology came in, those people moved to the technology rather than do film, but we still needed film so we didn't really lose that many staff. There was bit of natural wastage but no major changes really. It was still quite a large department: around 25–30 people in total. You had proper shift supervisors back then who'd give you an order for your jobs, we had proof-readers, who would sit and read everything.

Like close-reading text?

Every job was read. Even electronic jobs. We had two full-time proof-readers who sat there all day long reading ozalids and print-outs. And that was a huge bottleneck. You could put a job in there and you wouldn't see it for a week. They had hundreds of job sitting in there to read. And then it went down to just one reader and eventually the readers went. The first thing to go really were the readers. You've got to rely on your electronic files at some point.

It was still proofed out to the customer as their responsibility to check it, but we had more faith in the systems. The thing is, with Imposition Publisher, because it was very reliant on the correct driver to interpret the file in the correct way, and back then files were very lumpy and convoluted, there was a lot of random stuff dropping out, especially with fraction work and maths work and stuff, there'd be characters just disappearing, purely because the driver didn't understand everything in the PostScript, so it needed to be read fully.

So, is that similar to the problem now with Kindle devices and our XML?

Yes. It can't either display the full font set or some of the special characters, it doesn't have them, or glyphs and that, it doesn't know how to interpret them – this is in 1998–2000 with Imposition Publisher – because it's all about the interpretation of files. So, until you really got pdfs coming mainstream, and you could actually see the file before you processed it, you could at least check it. Whereas, in the PostScript days, you had no idea what the content was, you see. So you couldn't really view it until it came out to film. And you didn't want to sit and read a negative film so you'd make an ozalid and then the proof-reader would have the joy of checking it. They were knowledgeable guys. Sometimes they wouldn't have any copy, they would literally just be using dictionaries and thesauruses, stuff like that, checking through, making sure the data was correct, the math symbols were the right formula… they were clever guys.

You say the customer: you mean the publisher, right?

Yeah, the publisher.

The customer to me would be the author. Do you think the author would have received proofs at that stage?

I honestly don't know.

So the proofing that was done here was done for the customer, basically?

We'd just send them to our contact, whoever that was, and they would circulate them to whoever needed to see them. Some stuff wasn't proofed. It was checked and read in-house. It was basically our responsibility to make sure that it was right, and print it. So there was a lot of onus on the proof-reader to make sure that everything was right. We'd get a PostScript file in, the customer has a laser print out knowing what it should be, and without someone checking it, literally, letter by letter, you're printing and hoping that it's okay, so that's why we had the readers. In the Drawing Office days, before they were part of Printing, they had a whole bank of readers. There must have been six or eight readers, reading all the stuff they were setting. And the files they were producing – they were reading all that to make sure it was all right to pass on to the printer. So then we were processing it and having to check that nothing had happened in the process to make sure it was still as it was. A very long process. Very long.

How much time was saved in that prepress process with the platesetters?

It was a big time saver. When you made a manual plate – negative plates – you're looking at six or seven plates an hour. By the time you've exposed your film, put the masks down, put it through the processor, cleaned off any film edges, maybe put it back through, you're talking maybe six-to-eight plates in an hour. Colour film, you'd be lucky to get one every quarter of an hour, so four plates an hour. Platesetters don't care if it's neg or pos, it all comes out the same way, pretty much. The Lotum was running, I think, about fourteen plates an hour. So, three times as fast. Your plate output goes up dramatically. Plus, you've only got one guy running it. You'd have four or five platemakers back then, making plates all day long. They might spend a whole day producing just forty plates whereas one guy on a platesetter would produce a hundred plates in a shift, so that's where it sort of hit first.

The guys who then retired from plating weren't replaced because we didn't need them because we had this device that could do three peoples' jobs in the same amount of time. Then the Magnussens, you're talking 24–26 plates an hour. So, you're doubling it again.

You say that was the beginning of the end really for staff levels in that area?

Yeah, because you had files being processed electronically. After Impact we got Prinergy in. Originally, Impact was tied in to Prinergy, as the imposition side, and then it went to Preps. So it's just an imposition package. It lets you impose the file, bring it into Prinergy and again, the guys would spend one-to-two hours imposing a job whereas it would have taken two days to plan it by hand. So, all of a sudden you've got a massive increase in the amount you can produce, for less people on imposition as well as plates. So, your staffing levels... automatically, you've got almost half the people there you don't need anymore. Yeah, that was the big start of the end, in that respect: you just didn't need as many people.

It's interesting to me. I've learned a lot just hearing that. I had originally thought that it was the WISIWYG breakthrough that would have started that.

It was the start. Taiga was very good but, as I said, it was complicated – we only had one Taiga station because they were very expensive back then. Comparatively speaking, it would have translated now... you're probably talking almost a million-pound investment in today's money. And this was more than ten years ago. A lot of money. A lot of maintenance required on the devices as well. There was a lot of regular archiving. The scanner drums had to be sent off every month to be re-skimmed to keep them clean. There was still a lot to do to keep it running, even though it was electronic. All WYSIWYG gave us was the ability to make sure it looked like what it wanted to be before we put it out to film. Because up until that point you were having to run blind to film. And if it wasn't right, you'd go and rerun it to film, which wasn't cheap. You might spend an extra half hour checking it, but once you ran it, that's it, it's done. Around 1998, we got an electronic proofing device. We got a digital chromalin machine. So you could send the files from Taiga to a digital proofer, a colour proofer, that was calibrated so you got accurate results, so even before you commit to film – you've got a proof now. So, again, that's a big jump forwards. Around 1998, 1999. Somewhere around there. But again, it was very, very expensive. Digital chromalins worked out at about £50 each, so they were very costly to produce. The inks were very costly, the media were very costly. It would take you an hour to calibrate the machine, because you had to read 256 patches one by one. It was very accurate. That was the first colour proofer, really. Then, when we got Prinergy in, we got two Agfa Sherpas, which were quicker, cheaper. Again, you could output to proof without needing to go to film. So that saved everyone's time, and saved a lot of money. I think the Sherpas were due to be paid back over two years at the time, and we paid back within six months because of the volume we were putting through them. They were literally run into the ground. We had them for three of four years until they just fell over. They were just running constantly. So, electronic proofing was a big thing as well. That's when we started to get rid of the readers: we didn't need as many readers anymore, because things were being checked and double checked on-screen. Prinergy would obviously let us view things on-screen, we could do a virtual proof on-screen, so the operator could check the files themself. They would run their own proof and sit and check it themselves. So, we moved away from having a full read on a job to top and tailing it. They would check the head, the foot, the line endings – the operator would do that, he would sign the job off – and then the readers were instructed to start topping and tailing instead of full reads, so everything was becoming more reliant on the file [being] correct.

So, when a reader is topping and tailing, what's he looking at?

He's literally checking folios, making sure it's the right page, the head's right, checking the lining. In was then a case that the real problem you'd face was reflow: when a file is reinterpreted through a RIP it can reflow, so he was checking that the line endings were as [per] the copy. You were pretty safe if you knew your line endings were the same: the content was the same. If you knew that your line endings were the same, the content was the same because if something's changed, you'd see that a line ending has moved. So that was speeding things up as well – we ended up with only one reader. And eventually he went. Just retired and they never replaced him.

From having about thirty people working on film – imposing it, shooting it on a camera, or making plates – in 1992–1994, probably by 2000/2002, say ten years, you had six people imposing text, we had six people doing covers, from scratch, so that was the amalgamation of the Drawing Office – they were taking a raw file right through to a finished file, we had four people scanning, and probably only about six or seven people left over doing film work. Everything has shifted to electronic. So, people who had grown up with film were then retrained in electronic. There's the guy who trained me on colour planning – he started when it was hot metal. So he's been through hot metal, seen the big change from hot metal to litho, trained me in film and then I ended up training him in electronic. He literally saw three completely different technologies working here. At least they retrained him. Because they had the skills and understanding. The end result is still the same: you still need to know impositions, you still need to know what to look for. It's still the same as it was in the film and camera days, you're just doing it electronically.

Is there anyone else like him left?

There's one, I think, maybe two. I think I've got two guys who are 'old school', from the hot-metal days. One of them used to be a comp[ositor]: he would actually make up the type in the cases. He didn't come through to Prepress until we got, I think, Imposition Publisher, so he jumped from doing that sort of work to imposing electronic files. He was a comp, originally. He's still going strong. The rest of us were all film planners, by training,. I learned hot metal at college, a little bit, but we [CUP] weren't doing it anymore. I touched on it, but we were primarily film brought up, from the early days when there were no devices. There was just a camera, tint-laying, contacting, duplicating film, that sort of thing. And one of the plate makers is one of the original plate makers from when I started in 1992. So he's seen the change as well. He's done plate making all his life, but he's now running a device rather than making plates manually.

It's remarkable to think of the volume of plates he's doing on a shift now, on his own.

Yeah, he's probably doing a month's production in a week now, quite easily. But, you know, you've got no plate-handling issues anymore – less chemicals needed…

Less dangerous too, I suppose, and more environmentally friendly?

Oh yeah. We used to have probably six or eight plate processors back then. We've now got two. A lot better chemistry as well. We're now getting ten thousand plates out of one bath whereas, back then, you were lucky to get probably a thousand out of a bath, if that. And you were constantly cleaning the processor. You were putting more through it and there was a lot more crap coming off the plates, basically. Plates are better now – everything's better now, basically. Apart from the skillset. To run a device now, you pick the job and you go 'make me a plate', and that's it. It's more mechanical now. He needs to know how to fix it if it goes wrong rather than anything to do with the plate exposure or an error in the file. If there's an error in the file, he goes back to the imposition guys and they put it right. But back then, if there was an error in the file, he'd get the film out and maybe touch it in with his opaquing pen, or he'd scratch something with a scalpel, or he'd lift the page and re-impose it to get it straight, and then make a new plate. Whereas now it's like, if it's a file problem, you may have to go all the way back to the typesetter. You could have just fixed it yourself in probably half an hour. That's the downside to it. If we had a letter missing, we could scratch it in with an eyeglass and a scalpel. Or if you had a scratch in a tint you would use a roping pen and you'd dot the tint back in yourself. Now, if you haven't got a source file, you've got to go right back to the originator of the files to get it resupplied.

You could doctor the print pdf, couldn't you?

Yeah, with the new technology, you can change the pdf, but if there's something fundamentally wrong with it, you've got to go right back to the source files. There's only so much you can do with a pdf. And it's dangerous, obviously. Oh, you can do more now with a file than you could with film, but you'd get round a lot more in the film days than you can, to a certain degree, now. That's the danger. You correct one thing and it messes several other things up. Back then, you might spend a day putting a job right, but you could do it in-house, yourself, and the job would go on the press the next morning, whereas now, if you make major changes, you've got to send proofs out, in case anything's changed. You've got to request new files, and it could be a week or something.

Would someone who has experience (of film) be more employable than someone coming out of college now, would you say?

I'd like to say yes but if I'm honest, I'd probably say no because I don't think that skillset matters so much now – purely because the onus has shifted back to the customer, or the originator of the file. It's like they're telling you the file's okay so you run with it. There are a lot of printers out there that don't check anything anymore. POD printers, for instance, or eBooks: the files going straight through to the end product. Everything's certified before you touch it, apparently. I don't believe it. I still think that when something processes, there's still a danger it can change.

Even pdf?

Yeah. pdf is just a PostScript with a shell wrapped around it, so you can see it. That's all it really is. PostScript is just code. If you take away the wrapping of the pdf, it's just a code that has to be rasterised when it's ripped so it still has to make that transformation. Obviously, with electronic products, it stays electronic, so it's not too bad, but if you're outputting to any sort of hard copy, it still has to be interpreted by a RIP at some point in its life. And that can still change. Something could go wrong. To me, that sort of background knowledge is essential more at a higher level. If you're going to have a full understanding of, say, colour, trapping, and processed files, it's good to have that background because the results are still the same.

But, in all honesty, if you came straight out of college knowing how to use all the packages, you'd probably stand a better chance than someone who has been in the trade for 30 years that can use them all but also still remembers when they'd spend all day making film. I think it depends on the printer though. If you're producing fast-turnaround, electronic products, one-off short runs, that sort of thing, then, yeah, I don't think it makes a difference. If you're doing a fine-art, high-end production, then I think those skills would be invaluable. Anyone can operate a computer nowadays but they don't necessarily know the ins and outs of why it's doing what it's doing, whereas this stuff gives you a good grounding to actually know how it's reacting... a pdf is still just a pdf: just a wrapped PostScript code. If you knew how to read code back in the day, you could go into a PostScript (file) and change things. If you do it now in a pdf, you're doing it visually only. If you change one thing, it's still linked to lots of other things inside that file, which can have a knock-on effect. That is the danger, because it is technically all one file and just because you think you're changing just that little bit there, because you can see it, you're still changing the file itself.

I think it's now a case where you'd always go back to the supplier, to resupply the other deliverables as well.

Yeah, that's the thing. If you're getting three or four outputs from the same source file, then you need to change them all accordingly.

Thanks, Noel. This has been brilliant. It's WYSIWYG what I will end up writing about, thinking of the eBook today, the problems I've been telling you about: Fractions, for instance, is a good example, not coming always through and so on. But that's more of a problem with the XML...

Yeah, but you see it's interpretation again, isn't it? That's the thing. Greek's another one that's always been problematic.

The interpretation by the eReaders?

Yeah. How the code is transformed into its output. It's still transformed into an eBook for mobi and the other types – it's still a different file being generated so it's still having to be retranslated to output to a different file format. So every time that happens, the background code is being processed in some way. I guess, depending on the limitations of the device, it depends on what it can and can't display. I mean, Prinergy, which is what we run now, is very... that was one of the big selling points of Prinergy, the whole WYSIWYG. As far as I'm aware, it's still the only system, from a printer's point of view, that lets you view a trapped pdf file.

What's 'trappped'?

When you used to work on film, if you had a blue and a yellow, for instance, you couldn't have them over the top of each other because you'd get the green line. So you would slightly spread one colour under the other. It's very, very minute but you'd basically do it with an extra foil between the two bits of film, just to spread the image or choke it slightly, to get things to fit. You obviously don't want the white key lines appearing. So if you have no trap on file, they call it 'butt fit', because it's literally: one thing stops, another thing starts. Because of the way everything develops and exposes, you'll always get a little bit of creep on your file. You'd get a white key line showing. One has to sit on top of the other, overlap slightly, that's basically [to] 'trap'. It's either choking or spreading – that's pretty much all it is. So anything that's more than one colour has got some sort of trapping on it where elements interact. Now, with Taiga you could see the trapping on-screen: you could manipulate it – you could see exactly how that output was going to happen because obviously it needs to be trapped to be printed. The same way with Prinergy, when it processes a pdf it traps it. So when you look at a pdf on-screen – you've probably seen it when we've sent proofs over, and we get feedback saying 'oh, there's a line between these two...' and it's the trapping line – because Prinergy actually puts the trap on the pdf. As far as I'm aware, it's the only system that does that. With other systems, it's trapped as it is output. So you never get to see it. So, by the time the plate has come out, you can't tell if it's right because you've got four separate plates – you can't see through them. It will have trap put on it but you won't know if it's worked until it goes on press. Because if you output four plates with trapping on, you can't see through them: you can't lay them on top of each other to make sure that they fit, whereas on Prinergy, you can actually view the traps on-screen and amend them if you want to. You can actually physically see, obviously at very high magnification – I think it uses 0.06mm, that's how much trapping it does. It's a tiny amount that you won't notice with the naked eye, but when you zoom in on that file you can actually see it. You can see the areas where things have overlapped, you can reduce it, change it, change the direction of the trap – for instance, change the colour of the trap. You know, when two colours meet, it gives you a new colour basically, and you can change that colour as well.

So, when we see trapping on the cover pdfs that get printed to laser and circulated, can we assume that will get taken care of?

Yeah. They have got trapping on them because the file was trapped. That's how we know it will print right. That file is the final file that will be output. It's not going to have anything else done to it at that point. Anything like that will just come right when it's printed. It's one of the things that needs to be there to give good printed results. Prinergy is very WYSIWYG-based as well. With virtual proof(ing) as well, you can proof it on-screen in its actual screen dots, so you're seeing almost the plate output on-screen, literally dot for dot on-screen. So you can check it that closely... if you want to [laughs].

Again, isn't that just the evolution of the Taiga, which is the evolution of WYSIWYG really?

Taiga was the first time I'd heard that terminology being used on a system. From a printer's point of view, or a prepress point of view, Quark isn't WYSIWYG. None of the packages are, because they have to go through changes before being printed. So, from a prepress point of view, until you can those changes on the file, that's when it's WYSIWYG. You're actually seeing what you're going to get when printed. You make something in Quark, make it look nice, and then the Repro and Prepress guys have to make it actually work. That was always the great divide.

That's because the Quark file will be interpreted again before printing?

Yeah, but it's also because they're just making something look good on-screen by putting different things together, but then all those elements have to interact to be processed and actually work when printed. There are only certain things you can print. Some stuff that comes out of these packages, you can't print in a million years. It's just impossible. For instance, they'll put layers on a file of transparencies, so on one page you can have ten different layers. Obviously, on a printing press, be it digital or litho, when you print one page you're only printing one page. All of those layers have to come down at some point and be squashed to print as one element. So, how do they all interact with each other, you know?

I thought that as long as it looked okay in the application file, it wouldn't matter?

No. One of the classics was drop shadows. When drop shadows were first used in things like InDesign and Quark, you could click on that and you can put a drop shadow on it, and a lot of the time when it was processed, it would look fine on-screen, you make your pdf, it looks okay, sometimes, but you'd get a white box behind your drop shadow. Because the idea is the drop shadow has got to overprint the background to make it look like a shadow. So, if you're overprinting on blue, you get a sort of dark blue fading back to normal blue. That's your shadow. But because it was an image being applied – the drop shadow is actually an image: once it's been processed, it turns into an image, basically – it was just going white behind it. So you'd get this nice, graduated grey tint of a shadow, but with a white background. And then when that finished, your blue would start again, so it would look awful. And it wasn't until it had been processed that you could see that. That was one of the biggest issues we'd face: files would come in and they'd look great, but as soon as you processed them, you'd get this white box appear around your drop shadows. It's just because it didn't understand the transparencies or know how to deal with them. That's why the Press uses Version 1.3 pdf, which is Acrobat 4, because Acrobat 4 didn't support transparencies. So if you make a pdf to 1.3 Version, it flattens it so the creator of the file can see what it's going to look like. Transparencies still cause RIPs problems, even now. They are still something that RIPs struggle with. The RIP has to interpret how it thinks it should look. No one's telling it. It's seeing all these special effects. It has to work out 'when I squash them all, how will they all react with each other and how are they meant to look?'. And it has to make that decision. Sometimes it works, more often than not it does, but there are times when the flattened result is not what the creator of the file was expecting. It could change the colour, the appearance of something, the shape of something...

Even as a pdf?

Yeah. Because a pdf can contain layers and transparencies.

I suppose I've been thinking of quite simple layouts.

It's usually things like covers, or complex colour pages, magazines, that sort of thing. A normal book, when there's just text and pictures – it doesn't matter because the elements aren't over-lapping. As soon as your elements are overlapping and reacting with each other, that's when a RIPs job is crucial, because it has to know how to treat those elements. At the end of the day, it's got to make just one flat element out of them. So it needs to know how to piece those bits together and flatten them all off. And that's the beauty of a WYSIWYG system. You can see what's going to happen to a file before you print it, or before you run to film or run to proof, which is obviously all costly.

That's really interesting. I'm trying to think ahead about how I'm going to write this up. I think we can end there. You've been so good, that was amazing.

***

Transcript of 2nd interview with Noel Robson
Wednesday, 4th April 2012
University Printing House canteen, 14.00pm

You mentioned last time that in 1998 the bulk of the text was still being done on cameras, shot on the Opticopy, with Taiga being used mainly for cover work. Surely, by this point, a lot of the text was coming in as DTP. Was it being run to film before coming through to you as CRC?

It was being run to CRC, we would put it on the Opticopy and shoot it to film. We were running film directly from files in 1998, from Taiga and Imposition Publisher, but the other stuff was still being pumped out as CRC, which we mounted and shot on the camera. All the text. The output from the Drawing Office was paper copy, and we were shooting this paper copy. It was late. We were behind the times here at that point. As I said before, I was using computers at college and we didn't have a single one here.

In what format were the covers coming in from the Drawing Office?

They were open files, so Quark and InDesign, which we would make print-ready: make the pdf, out them on Taiga, later on Prinergy, and run out film and later plates. That was one of the reasons we merged with them in the end. Their files were requiring so much work, it was easier to show them what we needed and the flip side of that was we could help them out with their work load as well. Instead of them making a file for us to rip apart and put back together, we just produced one file that went straight to pdf.

That they were supplying open source files for covers means that desktop publishing had impacted much more on covers than on text.

Oh yeah. Covers before that involved paper makeup and manual separation. It was a huge help!

Do you remember when the Opticopy came and went?

It was here when I came [1992] but it wouldn't have been in place for long. 1991, something like that. It was a fairly new thing – a proper imposing camera.

Presumably, it went when CTP arrived?

No, because we were still outputting film. We were dual-outputting a lot of film through the imagesetters. I think it was when we got the imagesetters in that the Opticopy was ripped out. That would have been 1998/1999, something like that. That was the first of the cameras to go really. We kept the Little John for a while, because we used to still do some of the Journals covers on that, which had always been paper makeup.

Regarding the files that were being fed in to the systems... Imposition Publisher, which you've already said was the big change, what kind of files were fed in to this?

PostScript. Always PostScript. You basically had PostScripts from every package out there, even LaTeX.

Would each page have its own PostScript file?

No, you'd have a PostScript for the whole job or in groups of files, like a chapter or 100 pages, depending on how they decided to output it. Then we'd import them in to Imposition Publisher but you had to have the correct driver for the correct package that made them because the way Imposition Publisher interpreted the file, it needed to know where it came from. So, if it was a Quark PostScript, you had to have the correct Quark driver; for TeX PostScript, you had to have a TeX driver, etc.

Imposition Publisher was just a software processing RIP basically, not a hardware RIP. You had to tell it the parameters of the file before you imported it. And it would do some funny things. Characters would drop out at the point it was being converted – the PostScript being processed – and you had no pdfs so you couldn't see what it was meant to look like.

Things like maths symbols would go to square boxes, just because the driver wasn't up to date. You'd have to go and update the driver and try again. Generally, you wouldn't notice this until you pumped it out on film, because you couldn't really view it that well on-screen.

So, the process of updating drivers and problems like drop out was improved by pdf?

Yes.

Was there WYSIWYG functionality within Imposition Publisher?

No. Taiga was the first WYSIWYG system. With Imposition Publisher, until you got the film out, you were blind really. So you had to check each bit of film really carefully. Painful.

The Harlequin RIP, its place in the process I don't quite follow. My understanding is you would prepare the PostScript files in Imposition Publisher, then send it to the RIP. Could you elaborate on this and the problems you mentioned?

Yes, It was a standalone box, basically. The problems were down to interpretation of PostScripts again. Because you have so many different types of PostScripts coming from so many packages, and only one RIP.

So even when it came out of Imposition Publisher, there were still interpretation problems?

Yes, it was still a PostScript. You'd import a PostScript in to Imposition Publisher and impose it, then fire out a PostScript from that to the RIP. The idea of the RIP being to turn it in to something we can read. Again, depending on the type of package, it would struggle with certain characters.

The drivers in Imposition Publisher handled the file, but the problem of characters dropping out was caused by the RIP, at the time. It was the sort of RIP that you'd upload fonts to as well. You could store fonts in the RIP, so, if a character was missing, you might have to manually install a font in to the RIP and pass the file back through again.

But you'd only notice the drop out on film?

Yes, or you might get 'various errors' on the RIP, strange 'PostScript error 23', for instance, and you'd then have to go online and look up what that meant, try and find out where that could be in the file. It was pretty unhelpful.

And this type of problem was remedied at what point?

Well, Taiga had its own RIP – it was outputting separately. Really, it was when we had Impact come in that we stopped using the Harlequin RIP. It was a good RIP but you were just throwing everything at it so you'd get the odd problem. Impact was another imposition package, the predecessor to Prinergy. We went straight from that to Prinergy. It was very similar, just good for handling oddments, multiset stuff, and so on. Imposition Publisher was fine if you had four straight Z's, but as soon as you started introducing half sheets, or oddments, it would fall over. Impact was more reliable.

The WYSIWYG aspect of Prinergy, it wasn't live, was it? Were you able to view?

You were looking at the processed file, the way you do now, how it's going to come out, at the resolution it will image at. After Taiga, that was the first time. It was a lot easier in Prinergy. The way it viewed, you could see the whole sheet rather than looking at it page by page, as you did in Taiga. It was all PostScript – pdf wasn't really any better than PostScript. Most people bought PostScript because all their systems could accept it. I mean, Taiga would accept pdfs and PostScript and TIFF. We used it heavily on covers, and it was linked to the big scanner as well so even though we stopped using it for imposing work, we still used it for the scanner. It used to scan a TIFF directly in to Taiga. You'd used it to make up covers and images. I think we had a split system initially. Covers were the first things to move on to Prinergy, because they were easier and had less pages to look at, and text followed about a year later. We had Prinergy for about a year before we moved text over to it. Text was still being done by Impact. Checking 32 pages on-screen makes it easier to miss things, compared to two pages of a cover.

From my research so far, it seems to me that the part of the

Press to benefit the most from WYSIWYG technologies is Pre-press, in that it made life easier and reduced error.

To rerun to film is a lot cheaper than redoing a plate. When we first went to CTP, plates were £10 each. So, a lot of money compared to a bit of film. It also meant that for the stuff that went through to the machine room, errors were reduced a lot. Instances where characters dropped out weren't noticed until the book was printed. You'd get a bound book and someone would notice that all the 'n's had turned into boxes, so you've got to redo the whole job. It put more pressure on Prepress because they were responsible for checking it, and as a result a lot of the checks in the machine room ceased because, apparently, there was no need for them. Machine down time was reduced: they stopped measuring sheets up. Every signature used to be ruled up and measured, they didn't need to do that anymore because we could do all that on-screen. Because whatever we had on-screen came out on plate – there was no chance of anything moving. It was all punched by the platesetter so was perfect fit. It benefitted the rest of the process, really. It just put more pressure on Prepress! The quality of the product improved. It was also a lot cheaper to put right. You could put it right within a few hours and get it back on press, rather than a few days or a week, if you had to go right back to paper makeup. Things like Taiga gave you the ability to correct the actual pdf file, so you could go in and tweak the file, make things right, without having to go back to the creator of the file, who might be on holiday. It gave printers the ability to correct stuff on the fly and made everything cheaper to put right. There was a huge period of time in which we were receiving rubbish. There was a period of around three or four years where mending so-called 'final' files was huge. We were putting them right daily.

Appendix E

On the introduction of computers to the design process...

In terms of actually producing stuff on computer and moving from doing illustrative work, which is what I first did when I worked at Addenbrooke's as a medical illustrator – we had very early Macs in the NHS in 1987, and I think those very early ones were SEs, and it was great because we had lots of things to attach to them in this 'age of change', so instead of doing things such as photographing all the drawings that I'd done to make slides for teaching, you would photograph them on to negative and then feed them into a thing called Imagewriter, which was basically a camera bolted on to the back of a plastic box that plugged in to your computer, the Mac, and you'd leave it running overnight, for hours and hours and hours, to do about twelve slides. And they'd come up on-screen, so you could do slide presentations on-screen. It was very limited: it was all black and white. When I was interviewed for my job at the Press, which was probably July 1989, maybe a bit before that, I turned up here and was interviewed by Simon Mitton, who was the editorial director of Science, John Trevitt, who was the Design Director – because the Press actually had a Design Director in those days – and somebody from Personnel, who I imagine was probably Christine Lawless, the manager of Personnel. So I was interviewed by a small number of people, and one of the particular things that was said to me was "You can use computers", to which I said "Yes, I can use computers". "You can use Macs" – "Yes, I can use Macs" – "Excellent. We have them! You can come and join us". After a bit of kerfuffle over getting the job, which was probably me just pestering really,

120

because I'd been offered a job at The Royal Society of Chemistry, as a book designer, but they only did about eight books a year and I thought that was pretty tame.

Do you know if that job was also going to be DTP?
I think it probably was. I do know that a woman who worked up at Addenbrooke's with me, whose name I can't remember, went to work there as an illustrator and she had used computers at Addenbrooke's so I assume it was the same kind of thing that I was [offered]. There was a little interim actually: I had worked at Blueprint between the NHS and coming to the Press, and they were a small publishing/print company in Cambridge, and that was all set up with Macs – as far as I was concerned, that's where you worked as a designer. You produced your artwork in black and white and printed it out to bromide, and then put it to board in the traditional sense of printing.

So you would use computers to make the black and white work, which replaced the activity of using Letraset, Letratone, and ruling pens, but if you wanted a colour picture or a black and white image as halftone/continual tone in the final printed product, you wouldn't do it on the computer. You'd print out to bromide, stick the bromide down on board, and then do the instructions for printers. It was done in stages. I'm absolutely certain there was this transitional stage where the computers were there as a tool, but they only replaced part of the activity of making artwork. At Blueprint, I did all sorts of things like invites, University Dining Club invites, and small A4, three-fold, two-colour, printed leaflets for things like – I think I did something for Thuddenham Mill, in Suffolk – and they were just graphic projects, but at the end of Blueprint, I did a 400-page medical book in Pagemaker, which was a long process, and that was my first encounter with a book. So when I was interviewed at the Press and I realised how many books they did in Science – when I started at the Press, I think, approximately, in any one year, a designer might handle 180–

210 books. It was a lot, but the whole number of books within the Science/Academic group at that time was only about 250. When I started at the Press, my contract was that I could do or freelance out covers but that with text, I had to design them. Everyone was mine. And that was a kind of schooling period of about two years, where the guy I worked with in Science, John Gray, everything he handled, he commissioned. So, basically, I was there doing everything he couldn't commission out or just in training, commissioning some things and he would do the rest. Because between us we had about 250 books, at any one time I either designed the covers or designed the text for maybe about 150 titles in that first year. He started me off really well on text design because we didn't use computers at all then. Even though, at the interview they had rather excitedly said "You use computers!", when I turned up, we didn't have any and it was at least six months before we got a computer in the department, and I think it must have been a Mac Classic or an SE30, but looking at the price of SE30s, which were 1MB, their new price in 1989 was $6,500, I don't think the Press would have bought them. I think they were more likely to have bought a Classic, which was about $1,600. They were in Production end of 1989/Spring 1990, when we got our first Mac in the department – maybe it was actually an SE30 because they were '89–'91. Very expensive. I remember when it arrived and Michael Holdsworth came in to the department with it and plugged it in for us, there was Pauline Ireland, who had become the Production Manager for Science after John Footer left – John Footer went to the Royal Society of Chemistry. I started on August 1st and she [Pauline Ireland] came around six weeks after that, so maybe late September, Pauline became the manager. She had come from Journals – This computer had been beamed down into the department and Michael plugged it in and it was turned on and we gathered around it. It was bizarre, because everybody kind of thought it was a bit like the Holy Grail, there was a lot of 'oooh'ing going on. That was the only computer we had for a

long time. I remember a very early database on it, a [book] record database, I don't think it was Filemaker but it was some system, and it was so basic that you could load the whole of the database on to a floppy disk and at the end of the day somebody had to put the floppy disk in, download the content of the computer and then keep it with them overnight, for safety! The next morning, they'd have to put it back in again and off we'd go. That was like that for a while. I don't know how long but I remember being told that if I wanted a computer – because I nagged to have a computer – if I wanted one, I'd have to go and sit at Simon Capelin's desk and use it when he wanted to use it so that he'd complain about me. That was my tactic for getting a computer. I assume he complained because I got a computer.

So, before you got the computer, how were you creating speci-men pages and layouts?
We were doing layouts much like this one I've given you, but at final size. You'd take A3 pieces of paper and actually draw out the page size. I had a parallel drawing motion board for doing this. You would draw a rough layout, pencil in where the back margins might go and start counting space using a points ruler, actually measuring it all out. At that time, you would measure out the layouts and design the layouts by hand, but in picas and points, not millimetres or inches, which is why, for me, the way that we work [now] with typesetters is a little bit odd because all of my schooling and understanding of how text lies on a page is in points and picas.

It's more natural to you?
More natural, yes, but actually it's considerably more accurate. What we might also do is ask the guys in Repro at the Printing House to set some text for us to strip in.

Is this when the manuscript has been copy-edited?

There was never any pre-production text work. Never. Mostly because copy-editing lasted about eight years and the drawing of illustrations could carry on *ad infinitum*, and a book would never go to a typesetter without everything [being] complete.

By typesetter, do you mean the Printing House?

Not always. Actually, one of the things that used to happen when a book came in to Production was the first person to see it would be the in-house designer, who would choose who the printer was, who the typesetter was, what fonts would be used, what trim page size it would be, what paper would be used and the manufacturing details – we'd do print and bind specifications at early stages – so, production editors and production managers would never choose any materials or suppliers, it would always be me. Depending on the subject, if the book was heavy in mathematics, we'd send it to somebody like Arrowsmith, who were down near Bath. But Arrowsmith priced themselves out of the market completely. I remember, it must have been 1993ish, it was £25 a page for type-setting an encyclopaedia of maths. We couldn't afford that. So, you would choose a typesetter: Servis, or Vision in Manchester, or Paxton Press in Suffolk, or Wyvern, in Bristol, Bath Press, and occasionally we used Graphicraft, which I think is in Hong Kong. I can't remember anyone else.

Each had their own specialities?

Yes. Wyvern were really general, very good quality – I think they were Linotype typesetters – Bath (Press) were general, Servis more complex – much like they are now, but they used to do lots and lots of series for us, Paxton Press always did the Society of General Microbiology because they handled it like a journal: we'd produce a chapter at a time; in fact we used to do that with a lot of series books where copy-editing would start – Society of General Microbiology was with Mary Sanders – and it would come out of copy-editing chapter by chapter and each chapter would go off to the typesetter's as if it were a little book. Because it was a contributory volume, each chapter would then go out to the contributor. Once they'd finished with it, it would go to the main editor, who would collate all of the incoming stuff and then send it back to the Press, fully marked up by the author, to go one by one to Mary Sanders. At that point, it would become a whole book. We did that with a number of texts. In those days, we'd do a lot of conference proceedings – work which we don't really do anymore but what one might class as slightly downmarket work – which we'd sell only to a handful of people who were at the conference or who were going to the next conference.

They'd generally be printed here?
They'd always be printed here. But we did typeset books as well.

Do you know anything about the typesetting that did take place here?
The only thing I remember about it was that they handled all of our CRC work because they had what I think was called an Opticopy machine and Ron Ireland, Pauline Ireland's husband, used to put all the stuff on Opticopy strips. They [Prepress] had great light tables on which they'd put all the film. The Technical Applications Group typeset a lot of books for us: more complex, larger format stuff and LaTeX – Alison Woolatt worked there as well. So, back to the layouts, that's where I started wasn't it? We'd produce layouts by hand and we'd mark them up much like this one here, where you'd have a hand mark up of all the marginal spaces, all of the printed, interior spaces, as in the type width and type depth: you might write little notes on there, and someone emulate really the way that Jack Bowls did it – I think that's the really nice thing about traditional book design. In my opinion, a good book designer enjoys using a hand and a pen as opposed to

a computer, which is a relatively clinical space, and emulating something you've seen that someone else has done by hand gives you access to the language of mark up and style of markup – the beauty in itself. For instance, where you might on one page, as we have here, have a type measure and then a type measure including the back margin, and also things that tell you how deep it is, and this lovely little curve around other lines here – I don't know what one calls that, it probably doesn't have a name – it's just a style adopted.

What I did was I looked at lots of old layouts and found a way of expressing myself by picking out the things I really liked. We'd do the markup for prelims on the manuscript itself at final design [stage] but in the earlier stages when you were doing layouts, there used to be on the title page a book, the logo was an actual open book with a little inscription saying 'established 1534' and I used to love drawing the book. I'd draw it again and again and again, and I could draw it without having any reference to it in the end. It was just a beautiful thing to draw. So, you would draw out all the pages.

A book would come in to Production and, much like it does now, it would go to copy-editing and after copy-editing you'd get what you'd call the preliminary design stage. In the very simplest way, a preliminary design stage would only be done to merely establish the number of words per page, so if a book was in a series, you wouldn't have a preliminary design stage because you already know how many words per page the book's going to have. We didn't have standard designs in 1990 – they didn't happen until about 1993ish. If a book was bespoke, which is anything other than in a series, you would need to draw up a specification for it. It might be based on something else, so you would draw up something of a similar nature, but the preliminary design stage was really important for that because it enabled you to choose the font, the version of the font – you know, is it a Linotype, is it a Monotype? What kind of version of Times or Baskerville?

So at this point, you'd know who the typesetter was going to be?

You'd have chosen the typesetter at the point it came in to Production. Quite often I would choose the typesetter based on how I wanted the book to look. If I wanted it to be set in Iridium, I knew that I could only send it to Wyvern. So if it was a Darwin College lecture series, I knew it had to go to Wyvern because they were the only people that held Iridium. And when they changed their system, there was another font called Iron, which was basically Iridium but under a different name. You'd know that you could stay with them because you knew you could still get what you wanted, but we'd have to change the specs to Iron and not Iridium. I think those were the two fonts anyway. So you would have to produce layouts and again they would be by hand, but they were very simple. And that's an enormous difference, [the] really important change that computer-based design has brought on is that, in an era when you're not using a computer – and the surrounding attitude is that this is a fairly hallowed activity, done by hand – the expectations are that you will only define a limited amount of information: you will have your page, your front and back margins, your head margin, which defines the text area, your foredge and foot.

You would then know how deep the page is in terms of lines of text, and how wide the text is, and what size it is. So, it might be 10/13 Times New Roman over 110mm (these days) and it might be 38 lines. So you have a 228x152mm book, approximately. But that's all you would define. You wouldn't say what chapter openers looked like, you wouldn't say what the part title looked like, you wouldn't say how the tables were filled in – none of that information, because, actually, preliminary design was all about the production controller sending that off to the person I had chosen to say "I've got this layout, can you tell me, with all of this manuscript, how long this will be?" and they'd do a character count on the manuscript and off it would trot. We very rarely get

127

suppliers [visting Cambridge nowadays] but it used to be that, and I can't remember the exact days, we'd have printers, particularly jacket printers, because most of our text was printed across the road at UPH, and we'd have typesetters come in. So, we'd have Alan from Servis and Terry from Vision, and Dave Green or Charles from Wyvern, Butler and Tanner, Richard Turner would come in – Paxton Press, I can't remember his name, tall guy, grey hair – and a number of other people. They wouldn't come in to visit the managers. They'd come in to visit the people they were working with, and they would sit at your desk and say "I've now got ten books with you, can we run through where they are, how they're doing? What service are we offering?". It would be a really hands-on approach – they'd come and sit down and talk to you. The production controllers were exceptionally knowledgeable in typesetting, the definitions of typesetting, so they would know what to expect and what to ask and how to ask for further things when they needed them. They'd be very knowledgeable about four-colour and two-colour printing especially, and generally, the printing and typesetting area[s]. One of the things the Press required they did was a print qualification. They'd do night-school printing, somewhere local. So that would be the initial stage where you'd produce this one double-page layout to get an estimate or extent while it would still be with the copy-editor. The copy-editor would markup by hand and the final stage of design would be... When I started at the Press, every book would go to Final Design, there were no exceptions.

Through just you and one other person?

Through me and one other person for Science books, and it was the same in H&SS. There was Jane Williams, Elenor Cole, Sue Watson, Helen Beach, and a number of other people over the years that worked up here – in total in the Academic group, there were six designers at any one time and they would each handle particular projects, from the start. You'd basically allocate them at the beginning, pre-copy-editing. When it came to Final Design, you would have this complete manuscript; a complete set of artwork. Well, a complete set of artwork that may be marked for redrawing, because at the point that it came in for final design, you'd start drawing the artwork, and it would stay in Final Design until the artwork was drawn.

Do you mean the in-house designer would draw the artwork?

Commission it. I had one once – Ayres and Loike Lignans – which was one of my first books, and it had chemical drawings – benzene rings, that sort of thing, and I sent it off to an illustrator, and it went back and forth, back and forth. What would happen is your copy-editor would have done a full markup on the artwork, on the roughs, because nothing was electronic: it was either sketches by the author or printouts by MacDraw, that kind of thing, or Chem-Graph.

You would send that off to an illustrator with a big long checklist, which would be the illustration number, documented by the copy-editor, and all the corresponding illustrations, with a label on so there's lots of cross referencing and safety in the process. The illustration checklist would have a number of columns which were unfilled and a final column which was 'final size', for the typesetter. And there was an area where the copy-editor could write a brief to the designer – just a little thing, saying "please omit such and such labels" – and there'd be some overlay to mark [for] the labels to come off. And the designer would send this package off to an illustrator with a fee, an order.

Then you'd get it all back, with all the drawn versions, and it would go back to the copy-editor, who would send it to the author, and they'd discuss it for a while and this would go on – *ad infinitum*. You'd get some corrections back and get them done until you had nothing to pass on anymore. Ayres and Loike Loit took six years. That is the most extreme I have ever seen, but quite often it would take five or six weeks.

Is that the bottlekneck that has been removed?

It's one of the bottleknecks that has been removed. It was very significant though. I would sit with 25 manuscripts on my desk; regularly I would have a New York skyscraper theme going on. I'd have labels on them all. John Gray used to have much the same. He'd have shelves with little labels on, saying where they were. We had file cards as, again, we weren't using databases, to track them. For about five years, I had little cards which I'd keep notes on. John taught me to keep notes in a particular way, using his shorthand that he'd developed over 25 years.

That's hilarious.

I know. It was fantastic. I kept those. By the time we turned over to computers, I had 750 record cards.

Did you commission much artwork from the UPH Drawing Office? What were they good at?

I did. They were very good at drawing illustrations. I did commission illustrations from them an awful lot. In fact, they'd be my preference because I could walk over the road, pick them up and bring them back. It was quick. They had a large drawing office. The manager was called Colin Yeomans and he had rows and rows of people drawing. They would draw on to board, then they would Xerox it, for proof check, eventually they'd put it on to bromide and the bromide would go to the typesetter, in big bags.

Via Production?

Via Production. Yes, because, by the time all the artwork was done and the final manuscript was marked up by Design, and the final type specification was complete, I would give the whole package to the production controller.

Who'd send it to the typesetter and the next thing that would come back would be galleys?

Sometimes it would be galleys, but not all books. Certainly not monographs, and not series books. You'd get galleys for books that were something like taxonomic lists or, occasionally, books that were in double column, the odd medical book. Actually, we didn't do medical books at that stage, but something, you know, of that ilk.

So what kind of proof output was it? A Xeroxed page?

Yes, much like what we have now, a Xerox page.

And that would by laid-out and typeset?

Yes, it was very similar to what it is now. In fact, to some extent, better quality, because you'd always get trims.

And, of course, the designer would have played a bigger part in the proofing that they do now?

Yes. The designer would always see all proofs.

What would you be checking? I mean, what would you expect the typesetter to have misinterpreted?

Well, I have to say that the standard of typesetting, in my memory, was better than it is now. The people who were typesetting, people like Wayne at Servis, could design. They knew how to letterspace small caps. The designer's focus would be on the quality, the finer points of typography. The letterspacing of small and full caps, setting numbers and text in lists, using terms such as 'clear for ten', so you'd know where the word hangs against the number, and just ensuring that the basic standards of the typesetting of typographic layout are met. Not heinous or awful things, like using sized full caps to try and emulate small caps – things that bring odd spots of black to the page and lose all the elegance and tone of correctly set text. You'd look for poor word breaks. Things such as the markup of proofs, or rather the details of the mark up of proofs, were far more, I want to say skilful, but far more... people focused on marking up proofs in the most communicative way, so that your typesetter would mark, before sending them out – I think it was in blue, your proofreader's marks would be in green, or typesetters' marks were in black, maybe. Corrections to where a typesetter had created an error were always in red, and your in-house corrections – "actually, I'm sorry, we'd actually like it to be like this..." would be blue.

So there would be communication via colour and, on top of that, the rather lovely copy-editorial/proof-correction marks would be used: deletions, expansions, italic; little wiggly lines under words – all very beautiful and quick-to-understand marks. And it seems to me that at some point we stopped using blue, green, red and black and now any colour goes. People mark generally in red because it can be seen. To me that just goes "how bad are these typesetters?" It just shouts awful typesetting when actually it might just be [non-typesetting markup]. I would sit with a blue marker and a red marker when I was checking proofs, and I would have to ensure that, every time I marked I'd have to be sure it was either a typesetter error or a correction.

And you had the top copy to check against?

Always the top copy would circulate round. I would be checking them [the proofs] against my layouts or the series specification, or a pattern book, and if I came across something that I felt wasn't quite right, I'd have to go and get a pattern book and have a look. This would be done as part of your daily job.

I imagine it would take quite a lot of time.

I'd say I'd spend two hours a day checking proofs. Of my time, it was a serious chunk. Sometimes, I would spend days and days checking proofs. There was this great job I did, which was

William Turner's *New Herbal*, which was two volumes and the first volume had already been published by Concarnet Press up in The Lakes. But we published it as a two-volume set. It was a boxed, large-format book, and an odd format as well: it wasn't a very wide book but it was very tall and thin. I had to go to the University Library to have a look at the original, which was around 1580ish. I had to go and have a look at it to determine whether we could photograph it, which we did down at the Library, and I got these bromides, 600 pages of bromides, of type that had been set in around 1580, where there was some drop out. I spent days and days touching it up with a rotering pen, filling in letters which had broken up, and I had to look at every page and decide 'if somebody chooses to look at this, will they be able to read it?'.

And the drawings, which had broken up through the wear over the years, I was building up – drawings of flowers – we didn't have the web to check it against, so I couldn't go online and check what the daffodils looked like. There was no reference like that. It was fantastic. Then Jackie Taylor designed the transcript in Stemple Garamond and it was beautiful. A really beautiful book. I think we printed around 600. They were terribly expensive. Those oddities came along, which we don't have anymore. They don't happen, probably because they're just not financially viable.

So, going back to the book at Final Design: you had it for preliminary design, copy-editing would have finished, and the quality of the copy-editing, to my mind, was, retrospectively, more detailed, more involved. The copy-editor would ask the author questions about the structure of the manuscript and the content of the manuscript. They'd be really involved in the book and I could ask the copy-editor questions like "what kind of book is this? What do you want it to say? How do you want the reader to read this part?", and they could tell me.

So, you'd have that kind of dialogue with the copy-editor at Final Design?

Yes, quite often we'd meet with them to go through the manuscript.

Would the author ever be involved at that stage?

Sometimes. Very rarely. We'd never show an author sample pages. In fact, there was never a stage like now, in pre-production, where some authors get lavished with tons and tons of sample layouts done on a computer. We never did that at all. I think it was because – and I hate to whinge – I think it was because there was this trust. Trust in the publisher, trust in the people the publisher employed, and trust in the professional who does their job. There were boundaries. Not boundaries that were "don't cross the boundary", but boundaries like "that's your job". So, I was left alone to design books and what I did was seen as the right decision because I had done it – it must be the right decision because the designer has done it.

And somehow that changed, I don't know when or how, but it changed. I do think that some of it is down to computers giving people access to [design], all sorts of things that take away from the process of making books: a respect of skills.

I know that skills change, or the requirements of what kinds of skills required to do different parts of the job change, but it significantly diminished the respect for what is an applied skill. It's one of the things that you continually battle against. People feel that if it's on a computer it's somehow owned by everybody. If it can be done on a computer surely anybody can do it. Whereas if it was done by pen on a bit of paper, people will run a mile: "I can't do that, it's drawing! I can't draw, but I can do computers...". I think that one of the great problems with 'DTP', and I hate the term, is that it diminished the quality of the work that we produce because it gives people access, people who don't really know what they're doing with text, people who don't know about letter spacing, spaces around em–rules, en–rules, when to use small caps, when to use old-style figures, when not to, when do you have a choice, what are the component parts of a font, how do I use them? What's a swash character? "Ooh, a swash character's nice and swirly. I'll stick one of them in at the front!" or "We'll set the whole word in swash characters!". People make the most heinous mistakes and they don't know that they're mistakes. By doing them, and somehow getting through to print, they're suddenly qualified to make that decision and it's right. But it's not right. There are two main reasons why it's not right, though it's not right on many levels, and they are, firstly, you can't communicate with people if you use type incorrectly, and the whole business of making books is communication, and the second is that we do have to give some credit and respect to the fact that people have designed fonts. Somebody, somewhere, sat down and drew an 'a' in Baskerville, somebody drew an 'a' in Times and they made the decision that this is how it looks, this is how it is to be used, and these are the basic rules that you can use this by. So we wouldn't take a section of the Mona Lisa and say this is a credible thing to do. We wouldn't because it's a respected image in its entirety. And a font is the same. All the rules that sit around how you use fonts respect the designer. So, I'm all for staying within decent typesetting rules, but they break them all the time.

And has that become acceptable?

It has become acceptable because – I don't necessarily know why but I think it's because access to typesetting is now the norm for anybody wanting to access it. People with PCs at home and some page-makeup programme and a font, they don't know what the font is, they got it free off the net, or it came with the programme, but it's jolly nice and they can read it. So they run a bit of text and do this thing called 'unjustification', stick a few pictures in and call it publishing when the truth is they've run it out as a pdf at some local printer. It's not published but they call it publishing and it makes them feel good. And I'm happy for them. People will make pamphlets for local charities and say "I've published this", because they made it on a 'desktop publishing' system, therefore "I've published it". It puts them in a place where they have no reference to what actually goes on, where they think the place they're in must be the same as what goes on in the business. There's nothing essentially very dangerous in that but it is something very frustrating when you find that all the skills you thought you could offer the world are suddenly 'owned' by a whole load of these people, who want to talk to you about it. You just want to tell them "but that's not right" and "I want to help you, but you're not willing to let me!". So you just have to close up and not do anything about it.

So we would do all this by hand, up to a point, and I'm not sure quite when we started doing layouts on-screen, but I know that it came no later than 1995 and the reason I know that is John Gray left in 1995, and I know that he wasn't doing it but Phil Treble started in 1995, and he was! He started in about July and he'd been to Reading University and prior to him starting we'd got Emma Smith working in H&SS and I think Emma was probably working in the remnants of Pagemaker in H&SS, but very soon after that we got Quark. I remember this enormous backlash against Quark because it was a 'new' programme that we'd have to learn, and all the Pagemaker users said they didn't want to use Quark but "No, you have to" said the Press, "this is the way we're going" and so everybody started using Quark and then said "isn't Quark wonderful!".

And then InDesign comes along and you get exactly the same thing, you know, backlash and then love. But sometime around 1995, layout on-screen started to happen.

So the very early design stage of a project, the comp spec pages say, would then be created in Quark?

Yes. We'd used to do one or two layouts for the whole text, by hand, and then mark up the hard copy of the preliminary pages, actually mark on it 'this is set in...' and scribble on the actual manuscript. So in this transition to making up sample pages on-screen, you would simulate that process but on-screen. So, you would have two pages of layouts and, possibly instead of marking up the manuscript, although I think I still remained marking up on manuscript for a while, if you had Word files, you would pour them in to Quark and lay them out there. And that's about the time we lost the little book on the title page as well, a blow for me. Now, for me, what happened after that is we started to lose control over what a book designer really contributes, and those boundaries of respect. Because as soon as you can do it on-screen, people stand behind you and watch you do it, telling you where to put it, you know, and that was very frustrating because they invaded your space.

Where you would be left to design and think and nurture something from within yourself to make a book that talks to the reader, suddenly, you'd have an editor on your shoulder saying "Can I just have the title a little bit higher? I think it would be better a little bit higher". And then gradually what you'd have was "Could we have a couple of more pages? Could you show me what a table looks like please? Can you run off another one? It doesn't take you long now". There were six designers. Whether the thought was "we have computers so we can start getting rid of designers", I don't know, but strangely enough, with more and more requests for more sample pages, electronic versions of covers, covers becoming marketing material in a way that they never used to be – because creating a cover took days and days before because there was no computer. You'd do it with sticky tape and drawing pencils. It was very complex. And you'd only do one! You were tired by the time you finished it! And had run out of ideas! There was this onslaught of "can we see this…", which developed at the same rate as we lost designers – people left and weren't replaced. By 2001, we'd gone from – I think we had seven at one point – from seven down to four. There were redundancies. In 2001 we had a thing called 'reintegration', where the H&SS and STM merged in to Academic Books. The department became 'Academic', but Production did this 'reintegration' thing, which basically squeezed out a few people, three of which were designers. And the number of production editors grew. We all had to reapply for our jobs and were told "these are the jobs that there are, apply for what you like". So, we ended up with four designers to do the whole of the Academic list, not specialising, so I've been doing the whole of the Academic list since 2001. I'd had a little tour of duty in H&SS before that, which I think was just a hint of what would happen from someone trying to warn me. We then had two people leave and they weren't replaced, so we ended up down to two designers for the whole of the Academic list. What happens in those circumstances is you have to be practical. You have to say: "Well, we only have this resource but we still have all of these books, actually, a growing number of books".

What we have in place now are mechanisms which either do or don't successfully manage books that either bypass entirely Design – that's why standard designs and series are handled in the way they are.

Meaning: no proof checking?

Meaning: no proof checking and no design. The idea of every book having Final Design, that went a long time ago. There just weren't enough people to do it. It was all rationalised. I think that the problem with that is that people see what is happening. They see a contraction of the number of people doing a job. Their expectations are that they will have these lovely sets of proofs because "that's what they can do". You've got this imbalance: they have less people but they want more. So how do you deal with that?

Outsource.

Exactly! You freelance, you commission and you buy things in.

You try to manage the detail that passes between those that want and those that produce. And that in itself is a bit complex. I think that's contributed to where we are with Design, which is everyone seems to have some ownership of it. My struggle is to continually try to keep ownership of design in Design. Not by excluding people but by offering things that are better than they can do, all of the time.

It's quite stressful because you always want to be better than anyone thinks they could possibly be. And a lot of people think they're really very good, including authors, and their nephews, and assistant editors, too. Today, I've got a marketer in New York wanting to take a text book cover to "have a tweak" so the person who's just spent days doing the visuals… it's just so hurtful. Completely demoralising.

I spoke with Jackie (Taylor) yesterday about the Kipling edition, asking her "could you tweak the layout of the prose to make it a smaller book?". I felt terrible. She had chosen the typeface, I think it's Garamond, and had spaced it beautifully out according to the poetry… she was upset.

Absolutely, And you can see why. This cover in New York is one of hers as well. Of all the designers we use, she is one who is really, really good with type. She really knows what she's doing and has a great sensitivity about it. And of all the designers, they chose her. It's mortifying. I would like to see, and I think it is not unreasonable, that somehow there was a more common awareness of the contribution that designers make. It's a skill that others don't have. And it's a valuable commodity. You'll only notice it when you don't have it. People sympathise with me, but I don't think they realise how much it hurts! My hands are tied. I can make things better on a local level, and I can tell designers how to work, and I can monitor the quality that they put out, but I can't stop somebody bullying you in to making changes. It's an irrational conversation: "I say no, you say yes'". They say "I want it" but what they don't say is "do I need it? Is this the best option?" And those kinds of questions are really rare. I think that comes from [people] being able to go home and do it on their computer. It's the power they think they have.

Do you think it's a possibility for the short-term future, for 'design' to be removed altogether from the Design department, for the type of product we're putting out?

Of the diverse range of products that we're putting out, I would say that for some of them, you could do that. Absolutely. We could do the covers for monographs somewhere in the Far East and we could say "all the books we print at 600 or less are going this way, their covers will go that way". Monographs, we'll devise something more strict, so there'll be no variation. We'll be really pragmatic about it. We'll get it signed off at the top and we'll say "all monographs are to have 2/3 bottom picture, 1/3 top, text always ranged left and always in this font and the editors will live with it and the books will sell, it won't make any difference. And it will cost $50". We could. And with Medical, we'll set up a supplier for medical titles, we'll give all the medical titles to this one design company and they could be in the Far East, we could do the typesetting and the covers there. We'll just manage it to go out there. We could do the same with textbooks, to some extent. But actually they're so variable at the moment, it might be difficult. So, that's probably 70–80% of our books that we've just shifted out. We could. And that last 20–30%, the PEs [production editors] could manage the design.

If we were left with the bespoke and "nice" projects, then surely we would need somebody skilled?

Yes, but not necessarily in-house. You'd send all your work to Hart McLeod who would size themselves up to do all text designs and covers for that last 20–30%. "We'll do all of them!"

And they'll do them at bulk purchase. So, there we are, that's 1,100 books dealt with. But, do we want do it? Can we afford to do it? It's the set-up cost but also, can we afford the risk that the outcome will be costly? If people don't like it, how do we go back to where we were? You'd invest a lot of time and money. How do you bring it back if it doesn't work? And there's also the day-to-day running of the department. There's the 'feel good' factor. Those things which aren't really quantifiable but actually do cost. Like our relationships with Editorial and Marketing, our commitment to what Marketing's needs are, and the shifting needs of marketing. When you have people in-house and suddenly something shifts, you can say "I'll work a way around that for you. I'm here, I know what I'm doing. Yeah, we can do that for you". If everything is out[side] and Marketing go "Can we have this?", we haven't got anyone to work it out. So, the cost of employment in any particular area, and this particular area of Design, is how you apply the ability to change, to finance, to communicate, to negotiate, the hidden costs. I think that unless you have a person, or several people, doing that you risk the possibility of having lots of activities with people who can't focus on the one process. If you split all of your design amongst ten people, who has responsibility for it, and how do you all change? How, if there's a change in branding or process, do you all change at the same moment? If you have one person saying "I now need you all to change this", and they [the designers] have spent all that time working out what 'this' is, they'll get them to all change together. It's a cost. A cost that's worth having, to some extent. Design has been caught up in this change from applied, manual pen- and ruler-using, bromide-sticking skills. It has completely changed who people are. I asked people last night what had happened and didn't get very detailed responses, but Jackie Taylor said "Well, I left when we were drawing things, had a baby, and then came back and it was all different. And I had to learn it". She said she spent four days sitting at a computer, bleating, and taught herself to use it. It was the same with InDesign: we'd suddenly change direction or software and they had no choice if they wanted to work. I think this is why I can't remember key things, because actually, I just adapted to what was happening. I loved it when we used to do the hand-drawn layouts, but it was so time-consuming. But what that does do is give you status. You concentrate on what's needed. If what you needed at design stage when a production editor said "these are how many words it is having and this is the budget", there is nothing else necessary at that point, if you trust the designer to make a book that's correct for the market. And a designer should be able to create a book that's correct for the market.

At Final Design, you want something that the typesetter can use to make the book. There isn't really a need for all the superfluous fluff that we have, even in a time of "we need it for marketing purposes!". We don't market the book with content at that stage. People should be able to understand what a table will look like. They say things like "Do you think this is the right printout? Is this tone absolutely how it will be in the book?" and "This is such an inexact science!" and it's very frustrating, because there is never enough. There have been circumstances where people want whole chapters set. It's an eight-chapter book and you want one chapter set by a designer, at a cost of £200? It's not right. We're not going to do that. It would be far better value to get some sample pages that the typesetter can follow, get them to set a chapter! But we don't do that because people think these 'sample pages' are somehow free. So it has made an enormous difference.

And I think that the eBook will make a greater difference, because that's an unknown thing. It's not the printed word. Mrs Brown chooses which font she wants to use today to read her book. That just takes it way beyond anything a book designer, or graphic designer can take part in.

Until parameters are agreed perhaps?
Yes, until we can start designing for 'the 'e' environment', in a

different way. I think we have to make products differently, structure our products differently. We have to make 'books' that have multiple possibilities at the author stage and not try to have multiple possibilities at the production stage. It's the commissioning process that's important. How do you write content with the interests of educating people so that they can get the most out of each environment in which they'll see the content?

The print format being just one, if any?
Indeed. I'm inclined to think that things like monographs should either be 'e' or print on demand.

Michael Holdsworth said something very interesting and funny. He said when they (monographs) become electronic only, we'll be able to know how many times they are accessed, in Library's for instance, and it might cause some embarrassment when it's discovered that in the four years since publication, just three people have opened it!

It was the same person!

The author!
I think it will happen. I think it has to happen. What makes me wary is who reads monographs? Not so much how *many* people read monographs but *who* reads them. If a substantial number of people who currently read them wouldn't ever read them in 'e' form, then why are we publishing them? Maybe print on demand is the market for a monograph. Then we'll know if the set up costs are worth it. If there isn't a market there is no point. There was a discussion that book designers of the future will be producing fine-quality books, which will be the only books available. But there isn't a market that will allow all publishers to produce only fine-quality books. That's not how it's going to be. Who'd want a fine-quality production of [looks around shelves] *The Urban*

History of Britain? *The Urban History of Britain* has a future in one of two places, in my opinion: either in a mass Cambridge encyclopaedia of knowledge, whereby you download snippets of information from all of these books, and I'm all for that, or it will be written in a different way and it will be an 'e' product. Why would it be anything else? I think the future is not quite as rosy for the book as possibly some people are trying to imagine. I think that people expect too much too soon and are so very accepting of disposable information. We live in a time where the younger generation, and even some of the older generation, are happy to dispose of content as soon as they think it's in their head. They believe it will be out there, somewhere, forever, so if you lose it from your head, you can just go and find it again. And novels, throwaway novels, they should just be downloadable. They don't actually add value to your life. It's pulp fiction. And the more we produce educational material for the iPad, etc., for young people, the more they'll want it like that when they're older: they'll be used to it. I just don't think there's room for the hand-rending process anymore. But as a teaching process, there is. Just yesterday, I had three PEs come to my desk with questions and in each instance I reached for a piece of paper and a pen and drew out what they needed to do. As soon as I had drawn it, they understood it. With DTP, when you show people more and more things, the less they'll actually look at what is important. All they're doing is feeling good with the overall feel of it. They're not saying "is this right for the market, who's going to be using this?" – they're too consumed with how they feel about it. Whereas with that [hand-drawn layout], you have to concentrate on what's there. You have to say "Do we really need 49 lines? How are we going to fit it in…?" You ask all the structurally important questions. With the printed book, we're trying to present information for them to take out as quickly as possible. The means of doing that is to give a good grid, structure, formality, repeat layouts – full, comfortable space in which people can learn. If you went to a classroom to learn, where the desks and seats are all in line, and the board's in front of you, the teacher's in front of you at a big desk – somehow you feel that you've walked in to a learning environment. If you walk in to a classroom where the seats are on the floor, the desks tipped up and the teacher's playing a guitar at the back of the room, you'll wonder "how am I going to learn here?" It's exactly the same with a book. If it's confusion on the page, the reader will probably not be able to learn as much, if anything at all. We have books like that, where we try too hard to pander towards what we believe is the right way to make a book (as well as squeeze content in) and I think what we have to determine is "What is the right way to communicate? How am I going to put this content into a form that people can understand? How big do my A Heads have to be and how important are they?" You ask yourself questions to define the space, but we look and say "Oh, can we have a bit more tone? Do you think the numbers would be better in black rather than blue?" and I always say "Well, can it be seen as it is? Can I see the number? Is it in a place where my thumb will cover it up? If the reader is to use running heads as a reference, then page numbers should be in the running head. The people who read these reams and reams of sample pages we make for them rarely ask these questions. And that worries me. But maybe they won't have to in the future!

Steph, I think that's a good place to stop. It's been more than an hour and absolutely brilliant. Thank you.

I ranted.

I just hope I recorded it! I know it's going to be great. I learned a lot.

Appendix F

On being told that I have recently spoken with Noel Robson, who also started at the Press in 1992...

I did a lot of training with him on Quark and some things in Page-maker so I was showing him how to use it.

That's funny because he came from the apprenticeship at Anglia School of Art, where he was learning all these modern typesetting techniques, but then he came back to the Press and went a bit back in time really because it was still all photographic imposition and so on...

Yeah, because I started on the Macs in 1984, when they came out, in the States and from that point until I came to this country – I moved back to this country because my husband's British – I came back here and I was really shocked that I couldn't find anywhere that had Macs. They were all still doing photosetting, so it was a bit weird for me. I felt like I'd stepped back, and then I worked for a company that used to do a lot of work for CUP. I used to do a lot of typesetting for CUP at this other company, and from there I sort of got head-hunted to come here to start up the DTP section. Again, it was like stepping back again. It was really strange.

So when was that? You were called in...

1992. I joined the Press in 1992. I was actually offered a job in 1987, but I refused it because of how archaic it was at that time. It only had its own typesetting system. Its own unique typesetting system. We just called it 'the CUP unique typesetting system'.

146

I don't think it was called anything different. It might have been based on something, I don't know, but luckily I never used it. It was still in place when I started here in 1992.

So, I got head-hunted in 1992 to start up the DTP section, for Printing actually, and then things moved on from there, but when I started they had an artwork studio, using Illustrator – back then, Photoshop was in its infancy – they were using Illustrator, they were using FreeHand, and they were mainly using the Macs for that. They did have a couple of Macs sitting in a group they called 'the Technical Applications Group', but they didn't really have anybody that were typesetters. They were using the Macs but not really using them, if you know what I mean. They didn't really produce anything.

How was typesetting done then?

Using the CUP typesetting system. It was all unique to them. It was their own typesetting system. All went into tapes, things like that. I never used it because I was brought in to set up the DTP section, but when I started... Bibles – it was quite funny because that was one of the first jobs I was brought in to do – it was the Bible and the CAMRA beer guide. So I did that. One of the things when I was actually interviewed was they showed me this book, a CAMRA book, and they said "why do you think this won't work well in our system?" and I remember looking at it and the guy who was interviewing me at the time, he asked me that question, and I said "well, it looks to me that you're going to have a spacing issue. You're going to need to space it out so that they (columns) all end evenly". He said, "No, with what we have we can't feather the spacing..." and I looked at him and I'm thinking "You didn't listen to what I just said to you, did you?" – because nobody had ever answered it. He just completely did not listen to what I said and just said "No" and the answer was exactly what I had just told him. We had been using Quark quite a bit by then, in the other company, and I knew what they were trying to do but couldn't.

Is this multi-column text?

This is two columns on one page, yes, and they're trying to make it even at the bottom, because otherwise, if you have set spacing, and headings, and you had little informational paragraphs, they all had their own spacing so, depending on how many lines you had on the page, they needed to make it even, look really nice and the CUP typesetting system couldn't do that. You had to manually put stuff in to make it work whereas in some of the DTP packages, you could actually ask it to feather-space things, you know, to the [text] depth. So I was a typesetter, and went from typesetting machines to DTP – but as a typesetter, so, by that time, I understood picas, I understood spacing, everything that they needed, I understood what they wanted to do. So, I was a typesetter coming in to this. Pagemaker was the first one that came out with page design, so in 1986 it was quite rubbish and finally they came out with a second version of that and then of course it started coming out as a typesetting package. Not so much illustrations, but a typesetting package.

Then of course, when I moved to this country, within a year or so of me arriving, Quark came out and hit in a big way. Now, as a typesetter, Quark was the better package for typesetting, because of the actual typesetting facilities we could use within it. As a designer – they didn't understand any of those rules, they just made the page look really nice – and what they used to do here, the designer would hand me a page they had done in Quark, and say "I want it to look like that". So I would have to strip out all of what they'd done, and put all the rules in, the style sheets, all the spacing, I would have to go and do that and set up a template and then use that template to run all the Quark copy in, the actual text, and start from there, and do the page layout that way.

Things haven't changed that much, have they?

No, not since then, but that was unique! Because in the old days, you would be given a spec, a written specification, which is what we would use to set up all our templates from there. And that was (hand)written. But these people, who were getting a chance to use these DTP packages themselves, they didn't want to do the spec, they wanted to do it all on [the] page. So they did all the samples: how they wanted the spacing, and so on, then we had to tear it apart and make a template from that. So that was where the big difference happened in that part of it. But when I joined the company, Bibles had never had text handed to them on a disk, they didn't know how to do that, so when I joined, I came to the first Bible I had ever worked on – it had already been done in Pagemaker by an outside supplier and I was brought in to make the next one, because we did a new bible using the (normal) page set up and then adding annotations and notes around pages, so they had a designer set that up, he set it up in Quark, and I had to actually make that work. And they were coming over with these disks going "can we use these?" – these Word files, text files – "can we use these to do this, without having to type anything?". I started as a manuscript typesetter, I used to type it myself, type it all in and then make it all up.

On what machines would that have been?

In the States, I was on a Compugraphic photosetter. Here, I started on an APL and the Miles program – there's another name for Miles, I think it's Miles 33 – and before I left the company I was at before the Press, we started on the Macs and then from there, went on to the Macs here. They got them in. That's what they wanted to set up. So, they were bringing these disks over and they thought "this is great, so different". So, I was taking their files and showing them how I could flow the text in to a template and how to make up and that's what they wanted me to do. In 1996, I think it was, they had a big event here, a big marquee and everything, for Bibles – they were promoting the bibles, and they asked me to bring my Mac down there and show them how we were doing the bibles today, compared to what it was before. To them, it was absolutely wonderful. When, last year, they were doing that Press History, when they asked people to help get the museum going, they asked me to be involved and one of the ladies who was from the original Bibles group, who took over Bibles while I was here, she came in and said "you want to talk to this one because she's the one who helped us move from this type of typesetting, bringing text in – she started that here for us" and I'm thinking "that's sweet". It was stepping backwards because we had already been doing that. It was also getting them to lose their unique typesetting system as well.

How long did that last?

It stayed up until they stopped doing typesetting altogether. It was still going in 2002, when they quit typesetting at Cambridge.

What was the (work) ratio between Mac typesetting and the Cambridge proprietary machine?

I'm not sure what the ratio was because more and more books were moving over to us and fewer people were needed in that area. But they did keep anything that was already set up for using that system – they just maintained those.

So, it was a capacity issue really? I mean, how many were you in the DTP section?

At our heyday, there were eight of us actually on Macs, from the DTP side of it, but there were also about five doing disk-conversions, and there were at least six doing TeX, because TeX was still being done in-house.

What was disk-conversion?

Part of that was moving it on to the other system. So we were taking the files, manipulating them, changing them so they could be used in the other system, the CUP typesetting system.

Changing from Word into coded text?

Yes. Changing to that system. We used to have a guy working on the CUP typesetting system, and what he did was work out all the coding for the specs on the unique typesetting system. They would have a print out of quite a string of code which was used in that system, and I remember him coming over to me when they decided to move some of the books they were doing in the old typesetting system over to the Macs, and I had learned what all those codes meant, and I then had to take them out and put them into a template on the Mac.

That is the reason why they set up the DTP section in the first place. At the time, we used to do a lot of outside work, and they [external customers] said "If you want to keep our business, you'll move (these over) to Mac. We don't want this to be on your system anymore, we want them to be moved over, so they can be used somewhere else, and not just on yours". So that's what they did.

Do you think Cambridge was behind the UK in that regard?

I do, yes. Definitely. It took them a while to move over because this unique system that they had, all the fonts were made for that system, but they knew, increasingly, that they had to move over, that things were changing, and that they had to do it. The other thing that they did is they brought Monotype in to take all the fonts that they had on the CUP system and create PostScript fonts from them, to be used on Macs. They spent absolutely thousands of pounds to have that done.

Was that the only way to do that?

At the time, yes. Truetype came a bit later. I think it was around but they weren't really using that, but PostScript is how they did it because it was specifically for the Mac. And that was great, you would have thought, but when you're flowing in text, and you're using a Mac font, the characters are there. So they asked me to use these fonts and try them. I started using them and all of a sudden I'm getting these holes, little boxes, all over the place, and to me it was amazing because you would have thought Monotype would know this, but they didn't know a Mac keyboard. For instance, if I was using a roman font, some of the characters such as the full point were on another set. So then you had to switch over to this other font.

Was that them being lazy in the conversion?

When I came in, they were just finishing the fonts. Within a month or two of me joining, they gave the rest of them to us. And I had to say "you can't use them" and they were upset because they had spent thousands of pounds to have this done. I think that Monotype took them literally. Because of the way they [fonts] work on their system, I don't know if there was naivety there, or whether it was on our part, but it sounds as if it was a little of both to me. So all those fonts didn't get used.

What a waste. So what was the solution to that?

We bought Mac fonts. We had to go out and buy them. We had no choice. Once we did that, the DTP section took off. As I've said, it started out with just me, and one other girl was moved over from the Pitt Building, so I trained her, and then, because more and more work was coming our way – because I had used to do a lot of CUP work, I knew a lot of people in Publishing here, who I used to typeset for, and as soon as I came in and started getting established, they started using us. So, a lot of work came our way because they knew that I knew how to typeset. They'd worked with me. That was one of the reasons why they brought me in.

So, Publishing wanted DTP to be used?

Yeah. And they started bringing designers in, who could use these packages as well. What they used to do was get their designers to set up the templates – some of these designers did know what they were doing – so they would set up a spec, and they would say how they wanted it to work, and then I would have to make up the template in, say, QuarkXPress, and then the book would come in to us. Sometimes I would complete the book and sometimes I would hand it over to other people to complete, but I would set up all the templates, get them ready for them. The lovely thing for them was that they were there and we were here, and they could come over and make sure they were happy with what we'd done, and say "yes, this is exactly what we wanted".

Quite a few of the books won design awards. So it was quite nice. It was good that way. When they decided to get rid of typesetting at the Press, a lot of people were upset about it, because it was convenient for them.

Was the decision purely financial?

I think so. I think, originally, they thought just about everything would go to India, for a lot cheaper.

But things had been going to India by 2002?

They had been, and we had a lot of Indians coming in to work on Journals, especially. A lot of the TeX work did [go to India], but a lot of the Learning, ELT and Education, a lot of it stayed here because of the nature of the work. The Academic titles were definitely going to India because they were just mono. That's how it worked. In some ways, it was a gradual change, and then they just made the decision to stop. And when they made that decision, we had to hand over what was left to other suppliers, especially the LaTeX work – they did hand over all that to India – whereas, with us, we didn't have to hand that much over in that way, they just started with new products. With Bibles, what happened there was, because I used to typeset all the bibles, we were in the middle of a couple of big projects and so I went with them to the supplier they chose and did the handover with them. They actually completed those books. We had them all set up, ready to go, and they just finished them. A lot of them were at what we called 'galley stage', some of them were still in the 'text' stage, where we were just getting the text ready, making all the corrections, etc. – we always did that as well – believe it or not, the bibles still get corrected. They do have committees that decide that that should be that. We still have some in-house that we have to help them do because they are ours in the first place, so we do still work on some of those. But mainly, at the moment, we just do covers for them but everything else gets sent out.

We don't do any new typesetting. We do help occasionally. In my team, I've got another typesetter in the group, so we both can help fix things if we need to, or finish things off if there's a real problem. But now, with the way we get everything in to the archive system, if they need to send them to somebody else, they can now. We still had the design team in the Pitt Building for a very long time, up until two years ago. A lot of their work was to do with marketing as well – they did a lot of stuff for the colleges, and they were the only typesetting we had left at the Press, and then two years ago, they got rid of them as well. It's all completely outside now. There isn't any typesetting actually done at the Press. There is some design, but not typesetting.

I suppose if there's a problem with a file now, it just goes back to the typesetter every time, because of the associated deliverables. You mentioned, when you were talking about Bibles, 'galley proofs' as part of the DTP process. That has slightly confused me.

In the old days, we used to do it and they'd strip them up. What they wanted is they wanted to see what the text looked like, even though it wasn't yet paged-up. But they wanted to see it, so sometimes, not always, occasionally, we'd put them in what we called a 'galley stage', just for them. So they can see the type, they can see what it looks like, and then they can start deciding how they're going to complete the book. Especially if they've decided that they're going to do a 'red letter' text, so they've got the same text, but they want to see the red lettering so it's easier to take that text, make a copy of it as a second set of Quark files, so they have two sets and can see what's been changed. It helped them and it's how they wanted to work.

So, there's still older-style things happening in Bibles. It's purely down to the way they want to handle the text. And then, of course, they start making up. And often, their files go out somewhere else to be proofed: specialists who read bibles. And when I started here, we had a complete house full of readers as well.

Could you give me an idea of numbers of staff because, on paper, you'd have thought – well, I naively thought – that when desktop publishing came in, out went the unique typesetting system, jobs were lost, new talent was brought in, but that wasn't obviously the case?

As staff left, they just didn't replace them. But then they started bringing in the redundancy packages, so we started losing proof-readers, but because less work was being done in house – I say less work, the type of work we used to do changed as well, because when we used to have proof-readers that would read everything, check all the style, and make sure everything was perfect, when DTP came in, that all went out the window. The spacing wasn't as important, just as long as it looked quite good.

Was that because the proofing was given to the customer then?

No. It was to do with the fact that it was a cheaper way of running the system. The CUP system was quite expensive. To do it as already made up, they could run it to paper, and they could check the paper, and a lot of the things we were doing were being checked by authors, and the people that were actually producing the book wanted to read it. So it wasn't necessarily being read by our people.

And also, what used to be accepted in the old days as rigid rules regarding how we did typesetting, started being relaxed when it came to DTP. So, like I said, the spacing wasn't as big an issue as it used to be. If you look at older books, you would see characteristics that are happening in the new books that you'd never see there. They would have things called 'rivers', have you heard of that? [Yes.] You wouldn't probably see that in an older-style book, but in the new books you would see that, and you'd have to accept it. You used to say that the same word couldn't end more than two (consecutive) lines – that all changed. Although we still tried to keep that standard going, but stuff coming in from outside didn't. A lot of the work was being produced outside of us and the quality was affected. If we were finishing it – because quite often, that's what happened – we would finish a title that came in. It might have been worked on by a typesetter but they asked us to correct it. Things like that, we would fix.

Things like final corrections?

Yeah. We would do final corrections in-house.

Would they finish their job by giving you a file that wasn't finished?

Yes. Well, for instance, if it did get read, and somebody saw corrections that needed to be made, instead of asking the typesetter to do them, quite often it would come to us because we were making the final file, the PostScript file, for printing. So we would do the last corrections. If we saw something that we were really not happy with, we would fix that. Unfortunately, a lot of the time, we just made PostScript files and sent them straight down. So that's why we'd get the final files, because we'd create the PostScript files or printing.

So those PostScript files were then sent directly to the image-setters?

Yes, well, they [Prepress] would take the files and change them so they could be impositioned in their programmes and then, from that [PostScript], it went to pdf and they could see what we could see, without having to rip it first. You were working a little bit blind with PostScript because it wasn't until they did the proofing stages, you know, print them, get them ready, that you could check to see if everything was okay. But when it came from an outside supplier, there was nothing you could do about it – there were widows and orphans, things like that, which were not acceptable by us, if we were doing it in-house, but we had to accept it.

So you would receive the Quark file, the application files?

Yes. With the images and things in it, and then we would create the PostScript files.

Making corrections if necessary?

Yes. If there were corrections that needed to me made, and if we found them, we would do it. Otherwise, we'd just do the PostScript and send them through. And then, when the pdfs started happening, again, they just went straight through to printing, to Prepress. We never even saw those. Until we decided to change the way we do things at the Press. And that's when Content Services was developed, so we could start those files, and now the final files come to us. We were mapped over on our skills to this new department. I went for ELT/Education because I always liked working with them and liked their books better, because they were more interesting [laughs]. Whereas mono books are a little bit boring and I didn't want to go in to Journals

WHAT YOU SEE IS WHAT YOU GET

either. I wanted to stay with them, and they wanted me to stay with them, as well, which was nice. I also inherited Bibles, even though they're an Academic group, I inherited them because they asked "Can Brenda stay with us because she knows how to work our product?". So that's why I do bibles as well, but it's really final stages now, so we don't see much. We will do checks on pdfs early on. A lot of the suppliers know us now and what they'll do is send me an email and ask "Can you check this, are we doing it right?" So a lot of suppliers know who we are and know that we'll help them. So we do that now. We'll do a check and the pdfs will go to final and be shipped out to wherever they're going to be printed – and, as you know, when I started here, everything went to our Printing, and now it goes all over. We send them all over the world now. That's the other big difference: you can see where things are dying out. Again, I think a lot of that is DTP because people can do it in their own homes, and they can hand you a disk with the finished files and there you go. And that was the really big difference as well: nothing went through like that before, somebody had to check them before they could go through. So, I saw photosetting – I never did work on hot metal, even though I'm in the right age group, because in the States it had already gone. So, when I was doing photosetting, people I know here were still doing hot metal. Just about all of those guys are gone now.

There's one, Noel says.

Oh yeah, well, maybe in the back. Maybe out back there is. But in our group there isn't anymore. So, when I came over here, photo-setting had started, but no Macs. That was a bit later.

I suppose the Macs came with you, pretty much, in 1992?

Well, I came in 1987, and they had their first Mac here, in the Artwork Studio. Like I said, they offered me a job, but I turned them down because I thought "umm, it's a bit archaic for me", what they were doing. They had got their first one in, and that was 1987. It was a couple of years later, around 1989, when they really started bringing Macs in, but it was really just for the Artwork people. They tried the typesetting, but didn't have the right people, until I joined, and then we set up that DTP section.

It's quite confusing, the evolution of the different sections. Was the 'DTP Section' the official name?

It was the Technical Applications Group. TAG.

What did that acronym replace? What was the department called?

No. it started as that department. They actually bought it out from another company. I cannot remember the name of the company, but they bought this company, and brought their people and stuff in.

So they had been outsourcing all typesetting?

No, it was all done in-house on the CUP typesetting system, but they knew they had to move on, so they brought in this little company as an applications group, but they weren't typesetters. Their hand was forced because their customers made them do it. Whether the Press would have done it off their own back, is another story. Eventually, yes, but probably not when they did. They were pushed in to it. What they didn't do was tell the people in the typesetting area, the CUP system – they didn't tell them why they were bringing me in. So there was a lot of resentment. They were scared. They thought I was taking their jobs away from them. What they didn't understand, because nobody told them, it was because their customers had told them [the Press] that "if you don't do this, we'll take the work away". And they were big customers, the Portland Press, people like that (McGraw-Hill?). They were big customers with a lot of books. The other thing that happened was, I was given a new spec and was told "set it up this way". This is what they wanted, the new customer, so we set up the new books and then we used to have two guys who used to run film – don't forget, we were still going to film then, either bromide or film, depending on how we were asked to do it – So one of the first jobs I did came out on bromide and they would take my bromide and hand it over to a makeup person, and that person was then stripping it down on the old blue grids! It was quite funny. One of the mangers in there, he came in to me, put this thing on my desk and said "You've done this wrong, you've changed the spec". "What do you mean I've changed the spec?". I didn't know they were still using the blue grids. I got them [the spec] out and I'm looking at the files...

What had he spotted?

He said it was "all out". That I'd got it [the spec] all wrong. So I went back to him, put it back on his desk and said "tell me where it's wrong". Then he went to the guy who had said it was wrong and they showed me these grids and I said "where did you get those grids?" and they said "that's what we used", and I said, "it's not like that anymore. We need a new spec". And they went, "oh". So they measured it all up and realised it was right! They didn't understand what they were doing. Nobody had explained. Communication was absolutely zilch. They didn't tell them what was going on. So, of course they were going to be worried,. Of course they were resentful. Later on, when they realised I wasn't taking their jobs away, we were keeping work at the Press, it all changed, and also a lot of their jobs changed. A lot of these guys were second, third generation. Then the Artwork Studio got bigger because more work was done there. Bureaucracy at the Press is amazing because when they brought me in they said "We're going to give you Illustrator", but when I got here somebody found out and I wasn't allowed Illustrator, or FreeHand, because the Artwork Studio, they would do all that. I wasn't allowed. I did get the programme, but I was only allowed to manipulate one or two things. I had to wait for artwork to come through them, they had to give it to me. We still had two separate departments, trying to work together.

Is this the Drawing Office?

Yes, it became the Artwork Studio. It was called the Drawing Office to begin with, sorry.

And then it became Repro, as we know it?

A lot of them went to Repro, yes, some left but the rest were merged in to Prepress.

According to Noel, whose take on time before the merger shows a huge divide of knowledge, the Drawing Office would be able to produce beautiful looking files but without fully understanding what they would have to undergo...

That's very true. There was a lack of knowledge at that time. Especially when I first started here, I would have to say "Actually, this isn't right". I was doing an encyclopaedia and some of the artwork was wrong, or something should have been done to it, so I just did it myself, which, if they had known, they wouldn't have been very happy, but I just thought "I'm not waiting for them, I'll just do it!" The team did get bigger, in the Artwork Studio, so there were more people, but still, they just did the same thing again and again, and then that job, once they'd finished it, they'd hand the files over so you were at their mercy, waiting for them to get it back to you. That's why we merged them together.

Were the readers a part of that office?

They were in that area, yes. Where all the Finance people are now. When I started, that was all the readers, the typesetting system, running the film... In fact, I'm now around three feet from where

I first started, twenty years ago. It was 'them and us', which was sad because when they realised that I wasn't the enemy, it worked out fine – we worked together fine – and we moved the Artwork Studio next to us, which was much better because we were then working together.

It was quite hilarious when one of the managers sitting in the typesetting part, he didn't want to have anything to do with us, because we were the new system, etc., and then one day, he came up to me and he handed me a disk and said "Could you just look at that disk – can you open it?" and I said "Sure. What is it?" He said "It's supposed to be Quark files but the Artwork Studio say it's not". So I put it in the machine, got it opened, saved it as a PC version and he said "Why couldn't they do that?" and I said "Because they don't have the knowledge, but they can". You'd try to tell them things but they were Old School: they didn't want to be told. For them, to move on to these new systems must have been hard – for some of them, because they were old guys, having to try to fit in. But some of them did do really well. The youngsters of course just picked it up and went on. I'm not from the computer age, at all. I came from the photosetting side of it, which was computerised, but it did just one thing; you could do fancy things, but as soon as you 'returned' it, it printed to the film.

So typesetting was finished in 2002?

Yes, because Content Services started in 2003. So there might have been a little bit left over from, say, TeX, LaTeX, and us, but the typesetting system was gone. They've still got all those things sitting in a safe over there. I don't know if you could read them but they've got tapes and things sitting there in the safes, from the unique system. We've still got floppy disks from when we started.

The Unique system is something I really don't know anything about. Do you know how that operated?

Yeah, if I can see if I can remember. How they used to do it is you would have keyboarders who would key, then you had these guys who couldn't key but could get it coded up, you know, get it ready, and they were the ones who would do the run of it. So they would run it so it went in to the pages. One cassette could do one thing, another cassette could do another thing.

Is there a galley stage?

I think, at that time, it had more or less gone WYSIWYG by then, with that system. But the way it worked was you didn't see it, you had to go back and go in to WYSIWYG and then come back out in to the code, and then go back to look at the page and then go back out, it was one of those systems. You couldn't do it as you were going along: you had to go in to that [WYSIWYG] mode. You would be coding, putting the text in with all the code, and then you'd go "Okay, now I want to see it", go into WYSIWYG to see what the page looked like. I'm pretty sure they could do that.

I didn't work on the typesetting system. I only know what the guys told me. It used to amaze me: they'd do the makeup but they couldn't type, because they had keyboarders who did all the inputting. The copy would come in, pages and pages of copy, and they would key it. And then, of course, all that changed when everything started coming in on disk.

So some of the keyboarders were moved to other departments, some left. They didn't really need keyboarders anymore. They did a little bit, for instance, some of the University work: somebody needed to key those in. So, the *Reporter*, or the Statutes and Ordnances, things like that, somebody needed to key in the bits that had to be included. So you did have somebody doing stuff like that but the keyboarding went. It was the first to go.

That's the advent of Word.

Yes, authors keying their own stuff and sending it in on disk. That had started when I arrived. People were saying "I've got this..." and they'd hand it to me for me to try it, a little floppy disk. Also, they didn't know that in Word you could do styling up that would carry over in to Quark, they didn't know how to do any of that. So I was showing people how to bring it [copy] in to a template. Nobody did any of that. They were behind in that sort of stuff. Very much so. Because, like I've said, they weren't really using Macs, they didn't need to, they were using their own system. They still brought text in through their own system but somebody needed to do the coding up. They couldn't just 'highlight', change to 'bold', you know, it was 'code, code, code, code'. I used to have some pages of some of the coding of the old system, that I had to change over to Quark. I'll have a look and see if I can find that. And I used to have some old notes and things for training people in Quark, and things like that. I'll see if I still have them but I know we did a big clear out last year and a lot of things got chucked. They might have too. I'll have a look. I think I still have one or two sheets from when Monotype changed our fonts over. We still use some of those fonts and that's because we have what we call CUP Pi fonts, little symbols, they could be Greek letters or little characters of some sort, like a star or something. We did use those because you couldn't always find them in fonts. You'd have to buy the fonts. And we already owned them so thought we might as well just use these. We might as well just use our CUP Pi fonts. Don't use them so much now, but we still have them. They're still legal. I'll have a little look through my drawers, see what I've got. We went from the floppy disk, of course, to zip disks, starting out at 100mbs, and the 250mbs, and then we went to the CD, and then the DVD, and the way we used to archive was on DLT tapes, little tapes that used to back up all the computers every night. Until we had our new system, the Asset Store, and now CAMS. The Asset Store was developed in 1999/2000.

This really is fascinating to me, the history, it's so recent.

Yes, it is. And it's moved so quickly as well. I mean, Prepress has really changed. I started when you literally burned it on to film first and then from film to the plate, I did all that, I started with that and it was still happening, of course, back then, so when it starting being computerised... I remember when I first joined the company, I had to go around and have what they called 'training days' where I went around to all the departments of Printing and met all these different people and one of the guys, he was second in command at the time, was really excited about going Computer to Plate. It was starting then. It was being developed then. He was really excited about it and was telling me "This is the future. This is what we're going to be doing soon. It's coming". It did take a few years. It would be around 1998, when we were doing PostScript. I remember him being so excited about it. And then a couple of years later he retired! I don't know if he ever got to see it, actually working at the Press. It was one of his babies, something he was trying to do, I don't know if anyone went to him and said "come and have a look". I always wondered... It was really amazing when I first started at the Press because there were so many people really excited about their jobs, and some that were literally counting the days until they were leaving. When I started, they had this one specialist bible printing machine, it was a beast, it was huge, because, you know, the paper was so thin, it needed a specialised press, and I remember meeting this man [press operator] and him saying "Two years, three months, twenty seven days" and I'm like "?". "Until I retire". [laughs] He'd been doing bibles for years. These guys were amazing.

Bibliography

- Adobe Systems Incoroprated, 2001. *pdf reference: Adobe portable document format version 1.4.* 3rd ed. [online]. Available at: <https://www.adobe.com/content/dam/acom/en/devnet/pdf/pdfs/pdf_reference_archives/PdfReference.pdf> [accessed 1/4/2020].

- Bain P. and Gennard J., 1995. *SOGAT: a history of the Society of Graphical and Allied Trades.* London: Routledge.

- Barlow G. and Eccles S., 1987. *Typesetting and composition.* London: Chapman & Hall.

- Black M., 1984. *Cambridge University Press: 1584–1984.* Cambridge: Cambridge University Press.

- Black M., 1992. *A short history of Cambridge University Press.* Cambridge: Cambridge University Press.

- Boag A., 2000. Monotype and phototypesetting. *Journal of the Printing Historical Society*, 2, Winter Issue, pp.57–77.

- Boiko B., 2005. *Content management bible.* 2nd ed. Indianapolis: Wiley.

- Burrows T., 1999. *The text in the machine: electronic texts in the humanities.* New York: Haworth Press.

- Coombs J., Renear A. and DeRose S., 1987. Markup systems and the future of scholarly text processing. *Communications of the ACM*, November, 30 (1), pp.933–947.

- Dobrowski A., 1991. Typesetting SGML using TeX. *TUGboat*, 12 (3), pp.409–414.

- Eliot S. and Rose J., eds., 2007. *A companion to the history of the book.* Chichester: Blackwell.

- Goldfarb C., 1981. A generalized approach to document markup. *SIGPLAN Notices*, June, 16 (6), pp.68–73.

- Goldfarb C., 1990. A brief history of the development of SGML, *SGML Users' Group*, [online] 11 June. Available at: <http://www.sgmlsource.com/history/sgmlhist.htm> [accessed 1/4/2020].

- Hendel R., 1998. *On book design.* Newhaven: Yale University Press.

- Jonason N. and Maeght P., 1991. *Pre-press (2): the changing world of pre-press systems*, [online] Darmstadt: IFRA Special Report. Available at: <http://www.wanifra.org/system/files/report/SRE2.03.06.Pdf> [accessed 1/4/2020].

- Kahn A., Lenk K., 1995. Screen typography: applying lessons of print to computer displays. *Seybold Report on Desktop Publishing*, 7 (3), pp.1–19.
- Lund P., 2007. Texts and Technology: 1979–2000. In: S. Eliot and J. Rose, eds. 2007. *A companion to the history of the book*. Chichester: Blackwell.
- Needle D., 2004. *Business in context: an introduction to business and its environments*, 5th ed. Andover: Thomson Learning.
- Oakley A. and Norris A., 1988. Page description languages: development, implementation and standardization. *Electronic Publishing*, 1 (2), pp.79–96.
- Oatridge N., 2003. Wapping '86: the strike that broke Britain's newspaper unions. *Coldtype Magazine*, [online] Available at: <http://www.coldtype.net/Assets/pdfs/Wapping1.pdf> [accessed 1/4/2020].
- Pfiffner P., 2003. *Inside the publishing revolution: the Adobe story*. San Jose: Adobe Press.
- Phillips A., 2007. Does the book have a future? In: S. Eliot and J. Rose, eds. 2007. *A companion to the history of the book*. Chichester: Blackwell.
- Pitti, D., 2002, *Introduction to XML*, [online] Available through: Institute for advanced technology in the Humanities, University of Virgina website <http://archive1.village.virginia.edu/dvp4c/xmlintro.html> [accessed: 1/4/2020]
- Pohlen J., 2011. *Letter fountain [on printing types]*. Köln: Taschen.
- Renear A., 2003. Text from several different perspectives: the role of context in markup semantics, [online] *Proceedings of the 2003 Conference on Computers, Literature, and Philology* (CLiP). Florence: University of Florence. Florence. Available through: <https://pdfs.semanticscholar.org/28da/afb0dfa6cb4c04cffaa02f42675cbf16c194.pdf> [accessed 1/4/2020].
- Romano F., 1996. *Pocket guide to digital prepress*. London: Thomson Learning.
- Seybold J., 1984. *The world of digital typesetting*. Media PA: Seybold Publications Inc.
- Shimada J., 2006. *The font wars*. [online]. Available through: Washington University website <http://www.cs.washington.edu/education/courses/csep590a/06au/projects/font-wars.pdf> [accessed 1/4/2020].
- Spring M., 1991. *Electronic printing and publishing: the document processing revolution*. New York: Marcel Dekker.
- Taylor C., 1996. What has WYSIWYG done to us? *The Seybold Report on Publishing Systems*, 26 (2), pp.1–18.
- Watson D., 2005. A brief history of document markup. *Circular 1086*, [online]. Available through: Agricultural and Biological Engineering Department, University of Florida website <http://chnm.gmu.edu/digitalhistory/links/pdf/chapter3/3.19a.pdf> [accessed 1/4/2020].

Notes

1. In 1984 the Press celebrated the 400th anniversary of its first publication, the *Two Treatises*, of 1584 (Black, 1992, p.57).

2. Experiments with photocomposition began at Monotype in the 1930s, with patents for the Rotofoto system of phototypesetting being filed in 1936 (Boag, 2000, p.58). By 1970, it had become the industry standard.

3. Offset lithographic printing was encouraged by the increasing demand for quality illustrative material, the creation of which represented an expensive and time-consuming procedure when accomplished with either letterpress or gravure technology (Seybold, 1984, p.400).

4. The laser printer was invented by Gary Starkweather in 1969 at Xerox and installed commercially for the first time in 1975 as the IBM 3800.

5. Digital typesetting, by which character masters were both photographically and digitally stored, is credited to the German company, Hell, which, in 1965, introduced the Cathode Ray Tube in to its third-generation machines (Seybold, 1984, p.113; Pohlen, 2011, p.29).

6. In 1986 Rupert Murdoch, whose News International organisation included *The Sun*, *News of The World*, *Times* and *Sunday Times*, controversially relocated its printing works from Fleet Street to Wapping, replacing letterpress printing with phototypesetting technology and enabling, for the first time in the UK, direct input of copy by journalists. The process famously saw the sacking of some 5,000 striking employees without losing a single day's production. He has been quoted by Linda Melvern in her book, *The End of the Street*, as characterising the manufacturing aspect of the industry in 1985 as "three times the number of jobs at five times the level of wages" (Oatridge, 2003, p.2).

7. Between 1988 and 1991 over 25,000 redundancies were reported by the British Printing Industries Federation. In 1991 alone, 200 British printing businesses closed and with them more than 1,000 redundancies were made (Black, 1992, p.56).

8. Total UK output: Books, Bibles, and Journals.

9. The other was Clays (Boag, 2000, p.73).

10. Out of frustration with how mathematical equations and technical documents were historically set inconsistently between output devices, Donald Knuth, a professor of Computing at Stanford University, created 'Tau Epsilon Chi', or TeX, as 'a standard, flexible, and extensible way to mark up a text file

with control codes defining every aspect of the typography of a publication' (Taylor, 1996, p.3). The open-source TeX macros utilise Metafont, a programming language used to define vector fonts from the Computer Modern family of typefaces and so, given the right macro package, the formatted output of two different TeX implementations on two different machines will produce identical results (Dobrowski, 1991, p.409).

11. Others include the proprietary 'CORA' code for Linotype and 'Troff' developed by AT&T for the Unix operating system, and Microsoft's 'Rich Text Format (rtf)'.

12. The GenCode concept was developed by the Graphic Communications Association (GCA) Composition Committee, which later became the GenCode Committee.

13. 'IBM GML' was published in 1969, four years prior to the public disclosure of 'GML', which, not coincidentally, comprises the initials of its three inventors: Charles Goldfarb, Edward Mosher, and Raymond Lorie (Goldfarb, 1990, p.1).

14. For example, a bulleted list within the body text of a document and a bulleted list within a boxed extract will both be given the same tag, but because of specification supplied by the DTD they can each have different styles imposed upon them (example taken from a presentation on 'DTD Notation' by Daniel Dunlavey, CUP, 2012).

15. American Standard Code for Information Exchange (ASCII) is a fundamental definition of the codes used by most computers to store internally such things as letters, numbers, and punctuation (Burrows, 1999, p.8). Each of its 128 characters is represented by a 7-bit binary number, making the code light and easily portable across devices.

16. HTML was originally developed by Tim Berners-Lee in the early 1990s at the CERN Laboratories, Switzerland.

17. ROCAPPI: Research on Computer Applications in the Printing and Publishing Industries.

18. It was the North American newspaper industry that, due to its inherent need for fast turnarounds, first drove demand in the early 1970s for significant graphic arts system development (Seybold, 1984, p.360).

19. At $17,000, the 1981 Xerox Star computer displayed bitmapped text as black-on-white and printed using Interpress, the Xerox PARC PDL. It was the first commercial system to incorporate a GUI, windows-operating platform, mouse, and Ethernet connection, and it inspired an industry before failing commercially.

20. In 1984 Hewlett-Packard introduced its Laserjet printer for the PC, which was capable of printing resolutions of 300dpi, producing near-typeset-quality outputs at a fraction of the cost of the alternative, 'daisy wheel' impact printers of the time. The first laser printers, conceptually introduced in the mid-1970s, were text-orientated and in the $500,000 price range. On

launch in 1979, Canon released its LBP-10 for $10,000. The HP Laserjet at that time cost $3,600 (Spring, 1991, p.171).

21. In commercial printing, in order to produce higher-quality images for proofing purposes, plotters are used, printing vector images – as opposed to raster graphics – based on the same laser-etching mechanism.

22. The Macintosh retailed in 1984 at $2,495.

23. The LaserWriter required extra processing power in the form of a 12Mhz Motorolla 68000 CPU, 512kb of RAM, and a 1mb frame buffer (Shimada, 2006).

24. The LaserWriter retailed in 1985 at $6,995.

25. Atex, a Kodak subsidiary, was a leading supplier of phototypesetting and page-layout technology to the US newspaper industry and, in 1986, equipped News International's aforementioned, controversial new Wapping print works (Oatridge, 2003, p.6).

26. The term 'desktop publishing' was allegedly coined by Brainerd himself, when asked to describe his company's new product ; however it is also credited to Jonathan W. Seybold in reference to a character from popular television programme, *The Flip Wilson Show*.

27. In 1989 Adobe released a Windows version of Illustrator for Microsoft, followed in 1990 by applications for UNIX, NeXT, and Sun SPARC workstations (Pfiffner, 2003, p. 87).

28. PhotoShop, created by Thomas and John Knoll, was in fact licensed in 1989 by Adobe as a companion programme to Illustrator.

29. 'Type 1' font format comprise two files: screen (bitmap) and printer (vector) outline fonts. The TrueType format contains its bitmap and vector information within a single file.

30. Display PostScript was co-developed by Adobe and Steve Job's NeXT computer company, following his acrimonious departure from Apple in 1985.

31. In 1994, Apple collaborated again with Adobe to develop its TrueType GX fonts and produced QuickDraw GX, an extensive graphics library that became a core part of the Mac operating system.

32. The technology behind the on-screen display of TrueType and PostScript 'Type 1' fonts evolved in conjunction with the personal computer's processing power, and with the incorporation of 'font smoothing' by Microsoft in its Windows 95. Font smoothing is an anti-aliasing technique that involves black, white and three intermediate shades of grey to smooth the edges of bitmap shapes, improving their appearance on-screen (Shimada, 2006).

33. Finally, in 1996, Adobe partnered with Microsoft to develop OpenType, a font technology combining aspects of PostScript and TrueType, to create enhanced fonts able to support non-Latin based alphabets in print and on the web (Pfiffner, 2003, p.65).

34. Phototypesetting was established as the offset-lithography prepress standard in the early 1970s, with the first machines being produced by Compugraphic,

despite its introduction as an alternative to metal typesetting in the 1950s.

35. In newspaper production, for instance, a separate typesetting machine would be used to set headlines, typically in full capitals.

36. Cambridge University Press was one of the first printers to incorporate the Monotype Lasercomp imagesetter in to its composition workflow. The other was Clays (Boag, 2000, p.73). Eventually, the Press ran three Lasercomp machines in its Composition department (App. C, p.70).

37. A combined weekly throughput of 2,880,000 characters. Based on the average book unit being 224 pages, each containing approximately 3,000 characters, this equated to an average of 4.3 book units being processed per week (Archive B, pps. 1–2).

38. For a standard book unit of 224 pages, each pass through the filmsetter required approximately 270 feet of paper or film (Archive B, p.2).

39. Letterpress composition continued as a Printing service up until 1982.

40. Wyvern Typesetting utilised a Linotype system offering a general, high-quality service; Servis Filmsetting, using a proprietor system, specialised in the production of complex layout as well as many AcPro series (App. E, p.124).

41. For example, the Darwin College Lecture Series was traditionally set by Wyvern Typesetting, who, as a Linotype typesetter, owned the series' consistently used Iridum font (App. E, p.124).

42. Standard designs, by which types of books not in a series, such as monographs and course books, are assigned a generic style and layout, thus streamlining the production process, were introduced sometime after 1993 (App. E, p.126).

43. For books belonging to series, an accurate cast-off could be determined at handover, based on the words-per-page allowance of the design spec.

44. Typically, this stage of the manuscript's preparation could last up to six weeks, a bottleneck in the production process resulting in queues of edited manuscripts surrounding designers' desks (App. E, p.129).

45. Neither method of typesetter proof output provided an entirely precise representation of how the text would be printed, due to the nature of the proofing system used. Bromide film would often contain blemishes and scratches symptomatic of the proofing process, rather than indicate faults in the master image, whereas photocopies thereof could distort the image slightly (Barlow and Eccles, 1987, p.222).

46. NB. In additional photocopies of this master proof, which would go to the publisher's proof-reader and the author, these typesetter's markings would appear in black.

47. The prepress and printing operations of the Printing House ran in continuous shifts, 24 hours a day, such was the volume of work coming through.

48. Prior to the widespread use of digital cameras c.2000 in producing images for 'reprographic' processing, continuous-tone illustrations were received and scanned as transparencies – high-resolution positive film such as those

used in projector slides. Between 1996 and 2000, the Prepress department scanned up to 10,000 images a year (App. D, p.93).

49. Colour work received from external typesetters would arrive at the Press in separated film, a 200-page book, for instance, requiring 800 individual pages of film to be impositioned (App. D, p.97).

50. In forming the TAG, the Printing Division acquired and installed in the Printing House an existing Cambridge company called Netherhall Software, which, in addition to devising off-line methods of disk-conversion, was experimenting with TeX and LaTeX typesetting (App. C, p.81).

51. Initially, 'floppy' disks had diameters of 8 inches, later 5¼", before becoming 3½". However, Amstrad disks were comparatively irregular at 3".

52. The Interset pagination system was trialled on the Society's *Fluid Mechanics* journal (App. C, p.78).

53. In 1992, Macs were already in place in TAG, but weren't used for typesetting. The Drawing Office, meanwhile, had been using Macs since 1989, utilising Illustrator and Freehand to produce artwork and corresponding PostScript files ready for press.

54. The Monotype font conversion was not successful due to the differences in keyboard configuration between devices. As a result, not every character contained in a given typeface's font was converted, leading to the TAG's purchasing of complete Apple fonts (App, F, p.164).

55. At its height in 1990 the Paper Makeup department employed eight dedicated proof-readers (App, D, p.102).

56. The Opticopy imposing camera could handle a maximum sheet size of 24x24 inches.

57. Trapping is 'the intentional overlapping of colours to prevent unprinted paper from showing in the event of misregistration' – i.e. the preparation for precise alignment of multiple printing plates on press to produce a coherent colour-printed sheet – (Romano, 1996, p.243).

58. Despite developments in imposition and, later, computer-to-plate printing, film plating carried on at Cambridge as a considerable amount of external work continued to arrive as camera-ready copy, in addition to any Publishing reprints, for which the original films were used. It is estimated that, in 2002, more than 50,000 titles were contained in the Printing House film stores, one of which was dedicated to external work, another to colour work and a third store was used for cover film (App. D, p.99).

59. The Littejohn camera was used for preparing cover artwork.

60. In 2002 the Prepress and Drawing Office merged to become one prepress 'reprographics' unit (App. D, p.95).

61. In 2001, the Prinergy system was introduced (as Taiga had been) primarily to process covers, while Impact handled the impositioning of text. Within a year, all text work was imposed using Prinergy, due to its provision of whole-sheet WYSIWYG representation (App. D, p.103).

62. On installation, the Lotum platesetter produced mono plates for the Speedmaster 2 printing press, colour plates for the Speedmaster 8, as well as four and five colour cover plates for the Speedmaster 74. In order to make plates for larger-format sheets, a Trendsetter was installed in 2002 and was fed directly from Impact. The next and final platesetting device to be installed was the Magnussen (x2) in 2008, capable of producing four different plate sizes at a rate of 24 plates per hour, running approximately 120,000m^2 of plate per year (App. D, pp.98–99).

63. By 1993, the volume of desktop publishing and TeX typesetting required nine operators for each system (App. C, p.81).

64. The first Cambridge journal to be published online was *Protein Science*, a proprietor-owned product, published in 1996 by the New York branch (App. B, p.71).

65. 975 new Academic Book ISBNs published through the Cambridge offices as of March 2012, with one month of the financial year left to run. Not including reprints, 'first time paperbacks', or electronic publications. Information gathered from the monthly in-house 'AcPro Titles and ISBNs report 2012' [accessed: 24/4/2012].

66. 444 new Academic Book ISBNs published through the Cambridge offices throughout the 1989 financial year. Information gathered from the Press' MAIDv5 remote Filemaker database [Accessed: 24/4/2012].

67. In 1989 the Press published the first of the Intergovernmental Panel on Climate Change (IPCC) reports, the content of which was created by the Met Office using Pagemaker. While the production process took an unprecedented six weeks, it required a substantial amount of reprocessing, due to its inclusion of multiple 'widows' and 'orphans' resulting from the source programmes' basic automatic pagination ability (App. B, p. 68).

68. Two of the six interview transcripts, those of Michael Holdsworth and Pauline Ireland, have been edited for reasons of sensitivity.

Index

www.ingramcontent.com/pod-product-compliance
Lightning Source LLC
LaVergne TN
LVHW022344060326
832902LV00022B/4236

*9 7 8 1 9 1 6 1 2 9 7 9 5 *